Written by
Máirtín Ó Murchú

The Irish
Language

*Máirtín Ó Murchú went to school
in Valentia Island and in Cork. After
taking an M.A. in University
College, Cork, he studied at Oslo
and Chicago before joining the
staff of the University of
Edinburgh's Linguistic Survey of
Scotland. He was subsequently
Lecturer in Irish Language and
Linguistics at University College,
Cork and was appointed to the
Chair of Irish in Trinity College,
Dublin in 1971. His primary
academic interest is in varieties of
the modern language and he is at
present preparing a detailed study
of the traditional Gaelic dialects
of Perthshire in Scotland.*

Cover: *Ancestral Head* by Louis le Brocquy.

Designed by Bill Murphy, MSIA MSDI
Colour separations and plates by Kulor Centre Ltd.
Printed by The Ormond Printing Co. Ltd., Ireland.

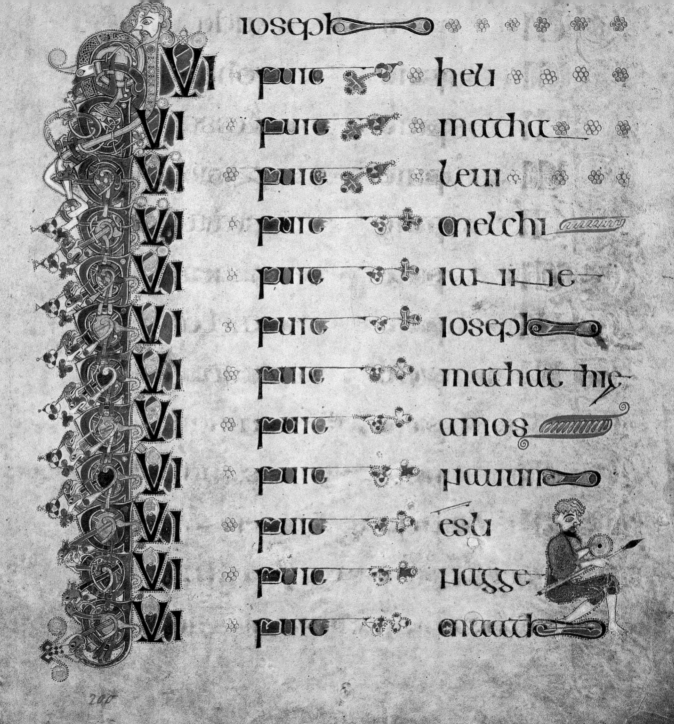

		ioseph
Ui	fuit	heli
Ui	fuit	matha
Ui	fuit	leui
Ui	fuit	melchi
Ui	fuit	ianne
Ui	fuit	ioseph
Ui	fuit	mathathie
Ui	fuit	amos
Ui	fuit	nahum
Ui	fuit	esli
Ui	fuit	nagge
Ui	fuit	maath

Contents

◁ 1. The genealogy of Christ, from St Luke's Gospel in the Book of Kells, the finest surviving example of the work of an early Irish monastic scriptorium, completed around 800 AD and containing the Latin texts of the Four Gospels.

Preface

Many of the cultural and population terms used in this essay have over time gone through considerable changes of meaning and at the outset, therefore, it may be appropriate to observe that:

(a) *British* is not synonymous with *English*. In most of the references here it describes the Celtic language and cultural tradition which was predominant in Britain in Roman times and is in later periods represented by Welsh.

(b) There is no universally acceptable single term in English for the unitary language and cultural tradition, the modern reflexes of which are Modern Irish, Scots Gaelic, and Manx. In Ireland the word *Gaelic,* which derives from the native term, has a distinctly pejorative connotation when used of the language, its use being intended to imply that the language is of peripheral status in present day Ireland. On the other hand, for reasons of contemporary politics, the Scots Gaels and Manx are not necessarily happy that earlier variants of their language are called *Irish*. I offer no solution to this problem but have followed what is customary usage in Ireland, and indeed in linguistic writing generally, and have used *Irish* as the term for all forms of the language except the modern Scots and Manx varieties.

I am most grateful to Liam Breatnach and Damian McManus who have been unstinting in their assistance; to Terence Brown, Proinsias Mac Cana and Helen Ó Murchú who read my initial draft and suggested many improvements; and to Aedín Ní Earchaí whose skill and patience ensured that the final typescript was in presentable shape.

2. A modern grant-aided factory in an ▷ Irish-speaking area of Donegal.

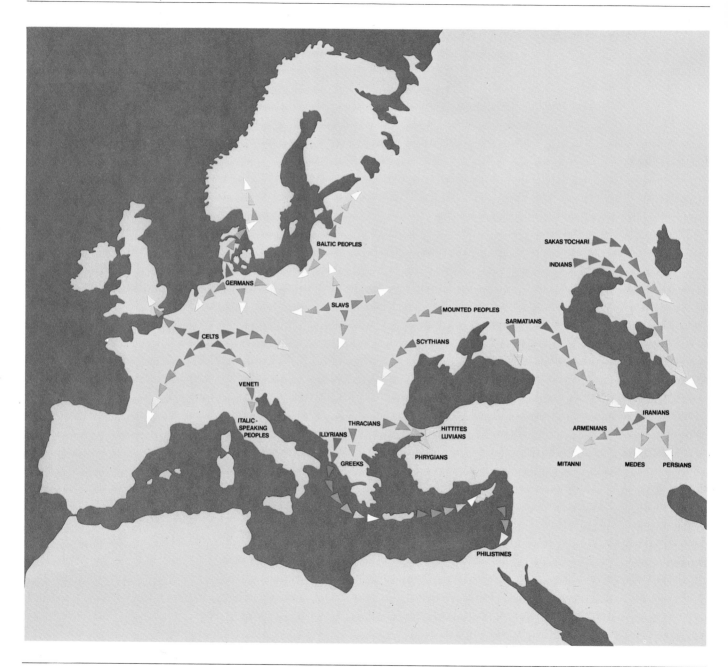

◁ **Map 1**

Expansions of the Indo-Europeans

1. Irish and Celtic

Irish is a Celtic language. So to describe it is to make an abbreviated statement about its origin and about its historic relationships to other languages and families of languages. In its grammatical forms and lexicon it has, for example, a much closer similarity to Welsh than to, say, English or French. It follows that for the discussion of linguistic relationships it is convenient to have a generic term for Irish and Welsh to express their closer affinity when compared with other languages. The term used is *Celtic*.

It is true that speakers of Irish and Welsh have not traditionally called themselves *Celts,* nor their languages *Celtic,* but the kind of systematic comparison which demonstrates the existence of a close historical affinity between Irish and Welsh reveals a similar affinity between them both and the language of, for example, the Gauls who occupied a substantial part of western Europe in antiquity.

Extant records of the language of the Gauls are meagre indeed but there is nevertheless sufficient information to set up comparative tables of words such as the one set out below:

That there is a similarity between the languages is obvious. What is more important philologically is that the similarity can be stated in terms of consistent correspondence patterns:

Gaulish has *a* where O.Ir. has *a* and Welsh *a*
Gaulish has *á* where O.Ir. has *á* and Welsh *aw*
Gaulish has *x* where O.Ir. has *s* and Welsh *ch*

If additional items of vocabulary are adduced, they conform to these patterns of correspondence which are therefore *rules* in the linguistic sense. The existence of such rules is the real proof that Irish and Welsh belong to the same family of languages as Gaulish; a generic term which might be used for the former two must also be applicable to the latter, or vice versa. Now the Gauls, according to Julius Caesar in his *De Bello Gallico,* called themselves Celts and they are frequently referred to by this name in the accounts of Greek and Roman authors. It was from these sources that the word has in recent times been borrowed to provide the necessary generic term.

A similar analysis of linguistic correspondences proves that the Celtic languages are *Indo-European* and thus share in an even older affinity with such ancient languages as Gothic, Greek,

Gaulish	Old Irish	Welsh	
carros	carr	car	'wagon, car'
cattos	cat	cath	'cat'
dúnon	dún	din	'fortress'
máros	már	mawr	'great'
nertomáros	nertmar	nerthfawr	'powerful'
uxellos	úasal	uchel	'high, noble'
sextemetos	sechtmad	seithfed	'seventh'
vindos	find	gwynn	'fair'

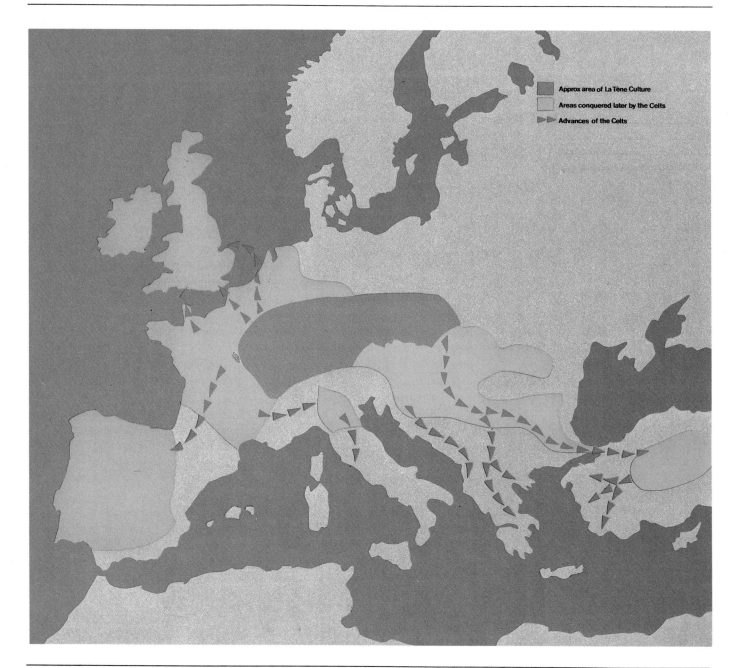

◁ Map 2
The expansion of the Celts

Hittite, Latin, Old Slavonic and Sanskrit and, less directly, with modern languages such as English, Hindi, Italian, Russian. The feature by which the Celtic languages are uniquely set off from all others in the Indo-European family is the loss of *p:* in some phonetic contexts where other Indo-European languages have *p,* or a consonant derived from *p,* the Celtic languages have no consonant at all. For example, Old Irish has *athair* corresponding to Latin *pater,* English *father;* Old Irish has *nia* corresponding to Latin *nepos,* English *nephew.*

2. Celtic Migrations

The distinctive features of Celtic speech, as preserved in records of placenames, personal names and rare inscriptions, correlated with archaeological evidence and references by classical writers, enable the origin and early movements of the Celts to be traced. It would appear that, towards the end of the second millenium BC, they emerged as a culturally distinct people in the region which now lies across the boundaries of eastern France, northern Switzerland, and south-western Germany, and began to expand over the area of what is now France into Britain, and possibly Ireland, and southwards into the Iberian Peninsula.

From the same central region, aided by iron weapons and, it would appear, a new superiority in transport — almost all Latin terms for vehicles are of Gaulish origin, for example — the Celts began upon a new phase of vigorous expansion in the 5th century BC. In this movement they expanded again over the area of France and into Britain and also reached the Iberian Peninsula. This time, in addition, they were involved in an eastwardly movement through central Europe and the Balkan Peninsula as far as Asia Minor, and southwards into Italy. It was during this period that the Gauls in 390 BC inflicted their famous defeat on the Romans and sacked their city.

Evidence for this is, of course, fragmentary; particularly so in regards to the arrival of the Celts in Britain and Ireland. The eminent Norwegian scholar, Carl Marstrander, put the matter bluntly, but indisputably, when he stated that 'no source tells us when the Celtic people who in historic times inhabited the British Isles, came there'. Their arrival in a series of invasions is, nonetheless, archaeologically detectable and it can be said with fair certainty that by 300 BC, when they were extended from Asia Minor to western Europe, they were probably also dominant in Britain and Ireland.

At the period of their greatest expansion, there are already distinct linguistic divisions among the Celts. There were on the Continent *Lepontic* in northern Italy, *Celtiberian* in the Iberian Peninsula, and *Gaulish* in Gaul. Gaulish at that time, though, did not differ from *British,* the Celtic language spoken in southern Britain, and the variety might more accurately be described as *Gallo-British,* but this is not an established term. In Britain, in addition to the speakers of British, there were the Picts in the north, a powerful people about whose language, or languages, very little can now be said with certainty. It is clear from later evidence that the inhabitants of Ireland were by the early Christian era predominantly Celtic, but as we shall see having their own linguistic characteristics.

3. The Decline of Continental Celtic

Roman power began to expand in the 3rd century BC with the conquest of northern Italy. Subsequently, following the wars with Carthage, the Romans established control over the Iberian Peninsula and, by the end of the 2nd century BC, had begun to advance into southern Gaul. Between 58 and 51 BC the conquest of Gaul was completed by Julius Caesar who also undertook two expeditions against southern Britain. The greater part of Britain was eventually brought under Roman authority in 43 AD.

In all Celtic regions, assimilation to Latin language and culture seems to have begun almost as soon as Roman administration had been introduced. On the Continent, the replacement of Celtic speech by Latin had almost everywhere been complete by the second century AD. There may have been peripheral areas in northern Gaul and Switzerland where Celtic survived as late as the 5th century AD but, obviously, Latin was predominant as it was the language adopted by the Germanic tribes who, from the 3rd century AD, had begun to push across the northern frontiers. In Armorica (Brittany), where a Celtic-speaking tradition was revived by migrations in the 4th-6th centuries from southern Britain, there may well have been an unbroken linguistic continuity from Gaulish times.

The extant fragments of Gaulish — preserved mostly in inscriptions, placenames, and in references by classical authors — convey little of the range of Old Celtic culture, are too sparse to allow a detailed grammar of Continental Celtic to be compiled, and would scarcely be interpretable were it not for the continued survival of a vigorous Celtic tradition in Britain and Ireland. In Ireland there survive in Irish more extensive early records than for any other part of the Celtic world.

4. The Collapse of Roman Power in Britain

From the second half of the 4th century AD, the Roman position in Britain became increasingly untenable because of persistent marauding by Irish Celts and by Picts, as well as by Saxons and other Germanic tribes. Eventually, the legions were withdrawn in 410 AD and the island was left to its own devices. Unlike the Celtic regions on the Continent, Romanisation was not very advanced in Britain and independent Celtic kingdoms quickly emerged following Roman withdrawal. These continued to be harassed by the Picts and Irish. The Anglo-Saxons, who may have been settled in Britain as non-Roman allies, or *foederati,* before Roman withdrawal, began now with reinforcements from their kinsmen from the Continent to win kingdoms for themselves and, within a few centuries, had gained control over most of lowland Britain.

Initially, the Irish were equally expansive from the west. From the north-east of Ireland the Dál Riata (*Riada* in later spelling) were establishing themselves in parts of Pictland in the north of Britain and, in the south, expeditions from the south coast of Ireland were resulting in permanent settlements in south Wales and beyond the Severn as far as the Channel. Because of the relative chronology, it may well have been these settlements rather than Anglo-Saxon pressure which caused the British migrations to Armorica, which took place in the 4th-6th centuries as has already been mentioned. Cormac Mac Cuileannáin, king-bishop of Cashel who died in 908 AD, mentions these developments in his encyclopedia, *Sanas Cormaic:*

Ba mór cumachta Gaedel for Bretnaib, ocus ní ba luga do-threbtais Gaedil for muir anair quam in Scotia, ocus do-rónta a n-árusa ocus a rígdúinte ann; ocus bátar fon cumachta sin co cian iar tidecht do Phátraic.

'The power of the Gael over the British was great, and the Gael lived no less to the east of the sea *quam in Scotia* (than in Ireland), and their dwellings and royal strongholds were made there; and they held that power for a long time after Patrick's coming.' This assertion, written a considerable time after the period in question, is corroborated by the survival of ogham inscriptions in south Wales, Devon and Cornwall.

Map 3 ▷
The Roman Empire under Diocletian (284-305)

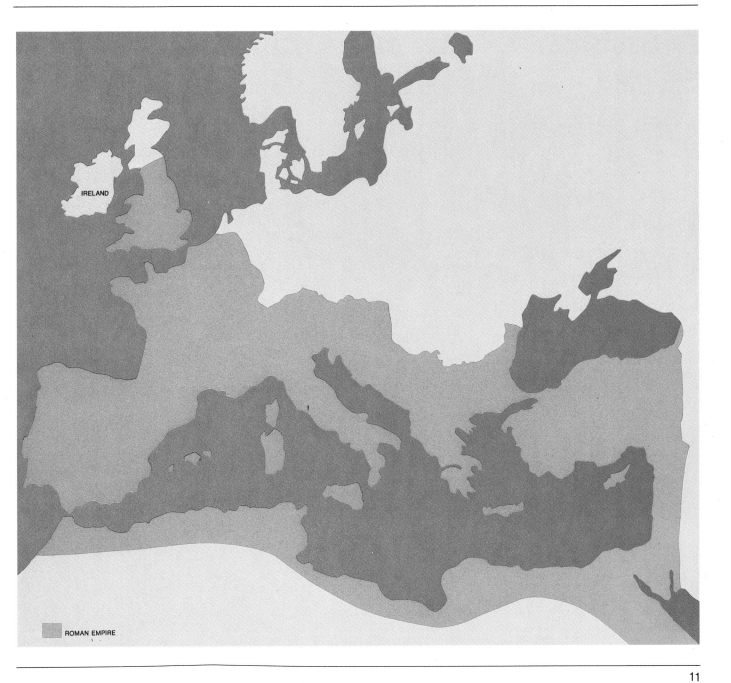

IRELAND

ROMAN EMPIRE

The Irish Language

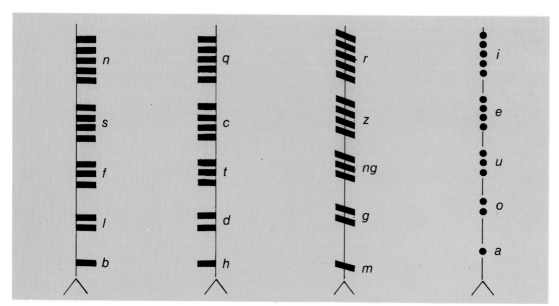

Ogham (*ogam* in earlier spelling) is a curious form of writing in which the alphabetic units are represented by varying numbers of strokes and notches marked along the edge of stone monuments; during its productive period it may also have been used for short texts cut on lengths of wood and bone. In origin the ogham alphabet is unlikely to be an independent invention; it is more probably a cipher based on the Latin alphabet, to which its relationship is comparable to the relationship which exists between the morse code and the modern alphabet. Native learned tradition may well have at all periods been aware of the correlationship between ogham letters and those of the Latin alphabet, and this may have been one of the influences which later determined the form which Irish orthography in the Latin alphabet took. Though the great bulk of ogham inscriptions belong to the 5th and 6th centuries AD, knowledge of the ogham script continued until Early Modern times. Its characteristics are, for example, described in a text included in the 14th century *Book of Ballymote;* the actual text, however, belongs to the 11th century.

In Irish, according to the statistics provided by R. A. S. Macalister in his *Corpus Inscriptionum Insularum Celticarum,* there are 369 known extant ogham inscriptions. Of these 121 are in Co. Kerry, where by far the highest density occurs; there are 81 in Co. Cork, and 47 in Co. Waterford. Macalister's map, though not very clear in regard to detail, effectively shows the striking overall pattern of distribution. The main thrust, starting in west Kerry, is eastwards through Co. Cork to Waterford, and thence across the Irish Sea to Pembrokeshire, where there are 15 — the next highest county density after Co. Waterford. The most easterly occurrence of an ogham inscription is on a stone found at the site of the Roman town of Silchester in Hampshire. This is mentioned in G. M. Trevelyan, *A Shortened History of England:* 'Before Roman Silchester was abandoned under Saxon pressure, an "Ogham stone" with a barbarous Celtic inscription had been set up in its streets, portentous to anyone who remembered what Silchester once had been'. To put the matter less emotionally, the existence of this inscription means that, after the Roman withdrawal, the town

Map 4

Distribution of *Ogham* Inscriptions
● Denotes single stones
● Denotes group of stones 2 - 5 in number
● Denotes group of stones more than 5

Scale
0 20 40 60 80 100 miles

at Silchester was occupied for a time by Irish speakers, not necessarily exclusively, until the area came under Anglo-Saxon control and the site was abandoned for good.

Since writing an ogham inscription must have been a specialist skill, applied only on behalf of individuals of wealth and status, stones are presumably found only where whole communities, or at least a secure ruling class, had been settled. Ogham appears to have originated in the south-west of Ireland, and it was there that it was for the most part practised. It is not, therefore, unreasonable to conclude that the geographical distribution of inscriptions, as portrayed on Macalister's map, is a fairly accurate reflection of the pattern of settlements made in other parts of Ireland and in Britain in the 5th and 6th centuries by people from the south-west of Ireland. In the north of Britain, of course, a much more vigorous pattern of settlement was being simultaneously undertaken by the Dál Riata of the north-east of Ireland.

5. Goedelic

Ogham inscriptions record a language which had preserved an older *kw (q, qu)* where Gaulish and Old Welsh have developed *p: maqq-*'son' in ogham, for example, corresponds to Old Welsh *map* (Modern *mab*). This correspondence is in itself of no special moment, since *p* and *kw* are acoustically very close, and frequently interchange in the history of languages, but it is a regular correspondence which provides a convenient criterion by which Celtic languages have been classified into two main groups: Gaulish, Welsh, Breton, and Cornish are P-Celtic; Irish and Celtiberian are Q-Celtic. Irish is also distinguished from the others, especially with reference to the prehistoric and early historic periods, by the term *Goedelic,* also spelled *Goidelic.* The word is based on one of the names which the Old Irish called themselves: Early Irish *góedel* (singular), *góedil* (plural). Interestingly the word is of British origin. The language was called *Góedelc* in Early Irish; the modern form is *Gaeilge.* The English *Gaelic* is based on the modern form.

It is not now possible to say whether the language which the Goedels brought with them to Ireland was already a distinctive variety of Celtic, or whether its distinctiveness developed in its subsequent isolation from the rest of the Celtic world. The fact that, in comparison with other varieties of Celtic, Early Irish is conservative, i.e. it preserves forms such as *kw* which have changed in the more central Celtic regions, argues for the former possibility, though not conclusively. It is at least not improbable that Goedelic evolved as a divergent variety of Celtic in Ireland and, if this is so, it is truly indigenous to Ireland and the terms Goedelic and Irish are interchangeable, even in respect of the earliest documented period. Moreover, although speakers of other varieties of Celtic may have settled in Ireland, when the historic period begins Goedelic is dominant and, except for individual words, is the only variety of Celtic encountered in Irish records.

3. An ogham stone in Co. Kerry. The script was usually read from bottom to top though it could also go in the opposite direction. Because of this, directional signs such as appear at the bottom of each line of the alphabet on page 12 were sometimes added.

3

6. The Golden Age of Celtic Ireland

Documents in Irish using the normal Roman alphabet do not begin until after Christianity had been accepted by the greater part of the people of Ireland. Omitting ogham inscriptions, the earliest contemporary records to survive are glosses and marginalia in manuscripts which have been preserved on the Continent. The most important of these are the mid-eighth-century *glosses,* or annotations, on a text of the Epistles of Paul in the Codex Paulinus at Würzburg, and the 9th century glosses on a commentary on the Psalms in the Codex Ambrosianus at Milan. This fairly substantial body of writing is the product of a culture which Christianity and Latin learning have permeated:

(i) although some native terms were available from the ogham tradition, a whole new vocabulary relating to literacy had been introduced into Irish from Latin;
(ii) religious and ecclesiastical terms had, of course, been freely adopted;
(iii) furthermore Irish society had been introduced to ideas and artefacts well removed from the core of Christian concepts and organisation (see Table 1).

As in modern literary English, all the words in an Irish sentence in these texts may be of Latin derivation:

ro-légsat canóin fetarlaici 'they have read the Old Testament text'; *lég-* from the Latin *lego; canóin* from Latin *canon; fetarlaic-* from an inflected form (e.g. *veteri legi*) of the phrase *vetus lex* 'old law'.

On the other hand, the traditional vocabulary may be entirely adequate for the expression of some concepts associated with the new learning:

ar-ecar a n-ainm i ndiúitius ocus ní arecar in briathar acht i gcomsuidigud 'The noun is found in simplex, and the verb is found only in compound'.

The monks who wrote the glosses sometimes digressed from their study and annotation of texts

Table 1

A sample of words of Latin origin in Old Irish (Old Irish spelling)

Irish	Latin	English
(i) terms related to literacy		
lebor	liber	book
légaid	legit	reads
líne	linea	line
litir	litera	letter
scríbaid	scribit	writes
(ii) religious and ecclesiastical terms		
aingel	angelus	angel
altóir	altaria	altar
bendacht	benedictio	blessing
caindleóir	candelarius	candle-stand
demon	daemon	demon
eclais	ecclesia	church
fescor	vespor	vesper
grád	gradus	order
ifern	infernus	hell
maldacht	maledictio	curse
oróit	oratio	prayer
peccad	peccatum	sin
relic	reliquiae	cemetery
ríagol	regula	rule
sacart	sacerdos	priest
umaldóit	humilitas(-atis)	humility
(iii) various other terms		
bárc	barca	boat
cathair	cathedra	chair
cucann	cocina	kitchen
metur	metrum	wooden vessel
muilenn	molinum	mill
saiget	sagitta	arrow
sorn	furnus	furnace
ungae	uncia	ounce

4. The monastery of Clonmacnoise, ▷ founded in 548 AD by St Ciarán, was one of the great centres of learning in early Christian Ireland.

4

to pen verses which they had either composed themselves, or were part of their contemporary literary repertoire:

Dom-farcai fidbaide fál,
  fom-chain loíd luin — lúad nád cél —
úas mo lebrán, ind línech,
  fom-chain trírech inna n-én.

'A screen of woodland overlooks me, a blackbird's lay sings to me — I will not decline to mention it — above my little book, the lined one, the twittering of the birds sings to me'. The fact is that these scholars were not succumbing to another, more powerful, culture. They were, on the contrary, the confident bearers of a vigorous tradition which, as they saw it, was through their mediation being enriched by the new religion and new learning. They were proud of the victory of Christianity and, with Oengus writing in the year 800 or so, could boast:

Ro-milled in genntlecht
cíarbo lígdae lethan

'Paganism has been destroyed though it was splendid and widespread'. They did evidently regard the native cultural heritage as worthy of interest and, as many of them were no doubt direct heirs to the traditional learning, it is not surprising that they devoted some of their new literary scholarship to making a record of the secular literature. The result is that Ireland possesses in the Irish language, as N. K. Chadwick, the well-known English scholar, says, 'a greater wealth of carefully preserved oral tradition from the earliest period of our era than any other people in Europe north of the Alps. For this reason the foundation of her early history from traditional materials is of general interest far beyond her geographical and political area, and second only to that of the ancient Greek and Roman world'.

7. Irish Expansion in Northern Britain

When the glosses in the codices of Würzburg and
Milan were being written, the Irish settlements in
southern Britain had been absorbed by the Anglo-
Saxon advance in England and by the
consolidating Welsh lordships in Wales. In the
north of Britain, however, Irish speakers were
destined to gain increasing cultural and political
influence. Irish migration to northern Britain had
begun even before the Roman withdrawal, but the
process gathered a new momentum with the
establishment around 500 AD of a small kingdom
in the part of Pictland which is now Argyll by the
Irish Dál Riata. In pace with Irish Christian
missionary activity, this small kingdom began to
expand aggressively under Aedán Mac Gabráin
who had become king in 574. Mac Gabráin was
eventually defeated in 603 by the Northumbrian
Aethelfrith and his ambitions permanently halted.

The influence of the kingdom of the Dál Riata must
nevertheless have continued to grow because,
around the year 843 AD, by a process which is
not now fully understood, Cinaedh Mac Ailpín,
king of the Irish-speaking people in northern
Britain, gained accession to the kingship of the
Picts. This must represent the final, rather than the
initial, stage of the adoption by the Picts of Irish
language and culture because by the end of the
9th century they appear to have been fully
Gaelicised. By that time, apart from peripheral
areas occupied by the Norse, all of the land north
of the Clyde-Forth line formed a unified Irish-
speaking kingdom. Later on, towards the end of
the 10th century the British kingdom of
Strathclyde, which had long successfully withstood
Anglo-Saxon pressure from the south, became
part of the Irish-speaking kingdom. Early in the
11th century the part of the Northumbrian
kingdom which lay north of the Tweed was taken
over. The southern border of the Irish-speaking
kingdom in Britain was now represented by the
line from the Solway to the Tweed. Although the
region was to undergo much further change in
language and culture, this has remained the
southern border of the kingdom whose name also
became fixed during the relatively brief period

10 0   10 20 30 40 50 miles

when it was predominantly Irish-speaking: it is called *Scotland* because *scot* (*scotus* in Latin) meant Irish-speaker in medieval times. (See Map 5).

8. Contact with the Norse

The Norse, meanwhile, had been encroaching on many parts of the Irish-speaking world and had made permanent settlements in the islands of Scotland, the Isle of Man, and around the coast of Ireland. References in the Irish Annals suggest that some permanent settlements were already in existence by 825 AD; by the middle of the century, the *Gallghaoidhil* 'Norse-Irish' were being mentioned. These were obviously a culturally mixed group, the emergence of whom indicated that the Norse settlers had begun immediately to intermingle with the local communities.

After 858, though this may be purely fortuitous, the Annals have no further reference to the *Gallghaoidhil* and they may have quickly ceased to be a distinct group in Irish society. However, the word continued in use as the name of a region in south-west Scotland where most of the population presumably was regarded as Norse-Irish in origin; the name survives in the Anglicised form *Galloway*.

In 1034, according to the *Annals of Ulster*, the overlord of that area was Suibhne Mac Cinaedha, *rí Gallghaoidhel*, unquestionably a representative of the Irish-speaking tradition.

Aided by such close contact between the Norse and the Irish, many words of Norse origin entered the Irish language during that period. They relate chiefly to seafaring and fishing, or reflect the Norse contribution to commercial development, but Irish contains many other words, which have been taken over from Norse but do not have such specific associations (see Table 2).

Table 2
A sample of words of Norse origin in Irish (Modern Irish spelling)

Irish	Old Norse	English
(i) Seafaring and fishing terms		
ábhar	hábora	rowlock
acaire	akkeri	anchor
dorú	dorg	fishing-line
langa	langa	ling
stiúir	styri	rudder
tochta	topt	thwart
(ii) commercial terms		
mál	mál	tax
mangaire	mangari	pedlar
margadh	markaðr	market
(iii) various other terms		
beoir	bjórr	beer
ceis	kesja	wicker
fuinneog	vindauga	window
iarla	iarl	earl
laincis	lang-festr	fetter
lochta	lopt	loft
pónaire	baunir	bean

5. The Gokstad ship was recovered in 1880 from a gravemound at Gokstad by the Oslo fjord. A fine example of a sea-going Viking ship of the kind used for crossing to the Hebrides and Ireland.

9. The Anglo-Norman Conquests

The political autonomy of the Irish-speaking people was at its greatest in historic times in the 11th century, after Brian Mac Cinnéidigh (i.e. Brian Bórú) had defeated the Irish-based Norse at the Battle of Clontarf in 1014 and Mael Coluim Mac Cinaedha, king of Scotland, by his victory at Carham on the Tweed in 1018, had consolidated his rule over the lands recently ceded by Northumbria.

The supremacy of Gaelic culture was not destined to endure for long in Scotland. The beginning of the decline there is usually associated with the reign (1058-1093) of Mael Coluim Mac Donnchadha who married an English-speaking princess of Wessex, Margaret. She was a person of powerful will who exerted an overwhelming influence on the ethos of the royal court. Whether at her instigation or not, Mac Donnchadha transferred his capital to Lothian, which can hardly have been completely Gaelicised even at the height of Gaelic power, and opened up the kingdom to settlers and traders from the south. The Gaelic language ceased from that time to be the language of court in Scotland.

During this period Anglo-Normans began to gain a foothold in Scotland. Gradually, they acquired estates, established boroughs, and in the process greatly reinforced the growth throughout the south-east of Scotland of a prosperous English-speaking aristocracy and burgher class. This English-speaking society was soon dominant in power and status, in control of burgeoning centres of population, and its influence rapidly increased. By the late 14th century the Gaelic language had retreated to the Highlands and Galloway, and was no longer regarded as the national language of Scotland. It continued as the vernacular in Galloway until the 17th century. After that, it was spoken only in the Highlands and regarded as something alien within the Scottish polity.

The Anglo-Normans became involved in Ireland in the late 12th century. It is well known that they first came as allies of the overlord of Leinster, Diarmaid

Mac Murchadha, in his dispute with the High King, but their arrival would not appear to have grieved other regional rulers who must equally have seen some local advantage in the development. When Henry II arrived in Ireland in 1171 various lords willingly submitted to him and, in traditional manner, gave him hostages. The *Annals of Loch Cé* give the following detached and brief account of his arrival and reception:

Ogus táinig i dtír ag Port Láirge ogus ro-ghabh gialla Mumhan; ogus táinig iar sin go hÁth Cliath ogus ro-ghabh gialla Laighen ogus fer Midhe.

'And he landed at Port Láirge (Waterford) and received the hostages of Munster; and then he came to Áth Cliath (Dublin) and received the hostages of Leinster and of the lords of Meath'.

The Anglo-Norman invasion gave rise to a new linguistic diversity as towns were expanded and new ones established, and religious orders, burghers and retainers brought in. At the outset, the dominant language among the new element was Norman French but this was replaced by English among town dwellers who, for longer than settlers in rural areas, remained unassimilated into the Irish-speaking community. The force and diversity of the Anglo-Norman impact on Irish society is reflected in the great number of words which entered the Irish language during that time. (See Table 3).

6. Cahir Castle belonged to the Anglo-Norman Butler family which was established in Ormond in 1185. The Butlers, though more consistently loyal to the interest of the English Crown in Ireland than many other Anglo-Norman families and slower to yield to Irish cultural influence, were by the early 16th century recognised as generous patrons of Irish learning and literature.

Table 3
A sample of words of Anglo-Norman origin in Irish
(Modern Irish spelling)

Map 6 ▷
The Gaelic world *circa* 1500.

This does not claim to be accurate in the detail. In particular, no attempt is made to represent areas or degrees of bilingualism precisely.

Irish	Anglo-Norman	English

(i) administrative, legal and military terms

Irish	Anglo-Norman	English
aturnae	aturnee	attorney
báille	bailli	bailiff
baránta	warantie	warranty
barda	warde	garrison
barún	barrun	baron
batáille	bataille	batallion
briotás	bretasse	brattice
buirgéis	burgeis	borough
constábla	conestable	constable
contae	cuntee	county
cotún	aketun	acton
giúistís	justise	justice i.e. judge
léas	les	lease
leiteanónt	leutenaunt	lieutenant
oighre	eire	heir
seiceadúir	executeur	executor
seirbhís	servise	service

(ii) architectural terms

Irish	Anglo-Norman	English
áirse	arche	arch
doinsiún	dongun	dungeon
dórtúr	dortur	dormitory
gairéad	garet	garret
pálás	palais	palace
póirse	porche	porch
seomra	chaumbre	room

(iii) terms for implements

Irish	Anglo-Norman	English
casúr	cassur	hammer
compás	compas	compass
gúiste	gouge	gouge
pionsúr	pinsur	pincers
siséal	chisel	chisel

(iv) various other terms

Irish	Anglo-Norman	English
ainís	anis	aniseed
asúir	azur	azure
bagún	bacun	bacon
buidéal	botel	bottle
buntáiste	(a)vantage	advantage
cabhalae	cavalee	hardship
clairéad	claret	claret
cúirtéis	curteis	courtesy
cúiste	cuche	couch
dinnéar	diner	dinner
fallás	fallas	deceit
galún	galun	gallon
gambún	gambun	gammon
gúna	gune	gown, dress
mailís	malis	malice
meadáille	medaille	medallion
milliún	milliun	million
pardún	pardun	pardon
pláta	plate	plate
saifír	safir	sapphire
siúcra	sucre	sugar
sólás	solas	solace
spás	(e)spase	space
spéir	(e)spere	sky
suipéar	super	supper
tuáille	toaille	towel

Next page
7. Tomb of Piaras Ruadh Buitléar (Butler), 8th earl of Ormond and Ossory and Lord Deputy of Ireland in 1528-9. By his time the Butlers were at their closest to the Irish tradition and a poem in Irish addressed to Lord Piaras has survived: *Mó sa chách clú Buitléarach* ('The Butler renown surpasses all').

8. An eighteenth-century engraving of Dublin Castle by James Malton. The castle was, for several centuries following the Anglo-Norman invasion, the headquarters of English administration and government in Ireland.

9. While the Penal Laws were in force during the 18th century, the schools which Irish speakers organised unobtrusively for their children's education were called hedge schools. Contrary to later belief they were probably seldom held in the open air.

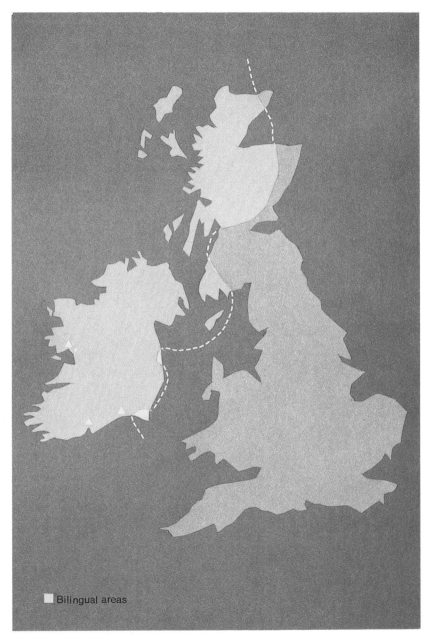

◼ Bilingual areas

10. The Gaelic Recovery in Ireland

The Anglo-Norman aristocracy, isolated in their rural strongholds, quickly adapted in language, though not to the same extent in political outlook, to their Irish environment. During the 15th century the boroughs, weakened by the Black Death and in economic decline, were gradually becoming Irish-speaking as well, though English was maintained as the vernacular language of law and administration. Attempts were made to stem the tide of Irish by passing statutes against its use, but these are probably evidence that the shift had largely occurred already. This is apparent, for instance, from a Waterford statute of 1492 which enjoined: 'that no manere man, freman nor foraine, of the citie or suburbes duellers, shall enpleade, nor defende in Yrish tong ayenste ony man in the court, but that all they that ony maters shall have in courte to be mynstred shall have a man that can spek English to declare his matier, excepte one party be of the countre; then every such dueller shalbe att liberte to speke Yrish'.

Irish thus, by the end of the 15th century, seems to have become the dominant vernacular in communities which earlier had been predominantly English-speaking or were expected to be English-speaking. There remained, however, a pattern of societal bilingualism, the details of which are probably not now determinable. The situation, as they encountered it during the 16th century, was described by various English officials who may be forgiven for misunderstanding the conventions of a bilingual community. Lord Chancellor Gerrarde, for example, reported in 1578 that 'all English, and the most part with delight, even in Dublin, speak Irish, and greatly are spotted in manners, habit, and conditions with Irish stains'.

This kind of report may contain some element of special pleading by officials who wished to emphasise the discomfort of their situation. Yet, in all the circumstances, what they report is plausible enough and it suggests that in the Pale, and in the main towns throughout the rest of the country, there was a pattern of Irish-English bilingualism in which the ordinary people were predominantly Irish-speaking and the aristocracy and better educated moved easily between the two cultures. Of the aristocracy more detail is, of course, known. William Nugent (1550-1625), son of the 8th Baron of Delvin, seems to be a fairly typical aristocrat of the Dublin Pale; he wrote literary Irish with a competence which can only have been acquired through a formal Irish education; he also studied at Oxford.

Thus had Ireland 'drifted back to its aboriginally squalid freedom' as *The Penguin Atlas of Medieval History* rather unsympathetically describes it. The Anglo-Norman invasion had been absorbed and, from the coalescence of the two cultures, a largely Irish-speaking early modern Ireland was emerging. Many English words entered the Irish lexicon at this time. They are often redolent of town life and sometimes reflect a colloquial English usage; some examples are: *airnéis* 'possessions' (Eng. *harness*); *cáipéis* 'document' (Eng. *copies*); *costas* 'expense' (Eng. *cost(e)s*); *geit* 'sudden fright' (Eng. *jet*); *ioncam* 'income'; *iontrast* 'interest'; *pionsa* 'fencing'.

The word *pionsa* should, perhaps, be more properly associated with changing fashions which, in that period, were another aspect of the influence of town on country, bringing further new words into the Irish language. Writing in the 17th century, the aristocratic Brian Mac Giolla Phádraig disparagingly describes in the following terms those who were taking advantage of the unsettled conditions to rise beyond their station:

Is gach mogh nó a mhac go *stairs* go hard le a
    smig,
cor tar ais dá *scairf* is *gáirtéar* air
is *stoc tobac* ina chlab dá lánséideadh,
is a chrobh ó alt to halt fá *bhráisléidibh*.

'And every peasant or his son with *starch* up to his chin, his *scarf* thrown back and a *garter* on, and a *tobacco pipe* in his jaw puffing away on it, and his paw from wrist to knuckle covered in *bracelets*'. All the key words are recent borrowings from English.

7

8

9

11. The Downfall of the Gaelic Polity

The period of Gaelic recovery was of short duration. The Tudor and Stuart suppressions and plantations (1534-1610), the Cromwellian settlement (1654) and, in due course, the Williamite campaign (1689-1691), and the subsequent enactment of the Penal Laws (1695) had the cumulative effect of eliminating the Irish-speaking aristocracy and learned classes and destroying their institutions. They were replaced by a new English-speaking landowning class together with an English-speaking middle class in the now expanding urban centres. The poet Dáibhí Ó Bruadair (1625-1698), echoing the sentiments of his dispossessed patrons, bitterly describes the confiscations of the great estates:

biaid ár ndúnta ag prúntaibh bathlach
líonta d'áirsíbh cáisí is praisce.

'Our castles will be in the possession of uncouth boors, filled with mounds of cheeses and porridge'. Efficiency, frugality, and insensitivity to Ó Bruadair's cultural heritage marked the new order. It was the end of an era.

In 18th century Ireland, as a result of these developments, English had, with very few exceptions, become the language of the upper classes and the sole language of government and public institutions. Irish remained for a time the language of the greater part of the rural population and of the labouring classes generally. It was not a period of unmitigated gloom for the language: the number of speakers began to increase again after the ravages of the 17th century, and there was a good deal of localised literary activity and extensive writings have survived in manuscript from that time. As the century advanced, and the Penal Laws were gradually relaxed, further change set in. When social and economic mobility improved, those of the Irish-speaking community who began to achieve prosperity adopted English as the language associated with, and indeed required by, their new status. The social status of Irish was thereby further diminished. This process began to accelerate after the Act of Union in 1801.

12. 19th Century Havoc

From the late 18th century the population of Ireland began to increase substantially. This increase occurred primarily among the poorer rural classes and, since a large proportion of that sector was still Irish-speaking, there was a disproportionate increase in the number of Irish speakers. There are no exact figures available, but in 1820 the number of Irish speakers was estimated at 3,500,000 and in 1835 it was estimated at 4,000,000. There had never before been so many Irish speakers and to friendly, disinterested, and hostile observers alike it appeared that Irish was making a massive recovery. With the benefit of hindsight, we can see the reality in starker clarity: these Irish-speaking masses were without economic or political power, and had no means of determining their own destiny. They had, of course, leaders such as Daniel O'Connell, or at a more local level the diarist Amhlaoibh Ó Súilleabháin, who fought for their civil and economic rights. Such leaders, though they professed an unfeigned emotional attachment to Irish, were generally willing enough to adapt to the existing pattern in which English was the language of politics, public affairs, education, and social advancement. In these circumstances, ordinary Irish speakers sought competence in English as essential either for social mobility at home or for emigration to better conditions in Britain or the United States. Even the most underprivileged sections of the community acquired more secure access to an elementary education in English after the National School system had been set up in 1831. This made it possible for them to switch to English and, after the trauma of the Great Famine, they had little hesitation in doing so.

It is not possible to state precisely what was the number of Irish speakers in the years which immediately preceded the Famine period (1846-8). An official census of population had been taken in 1841, but it had not included a question about language. Still, one has for the first time an accurate figure for the total population; it was 8,175,124. In the 1851 census the total

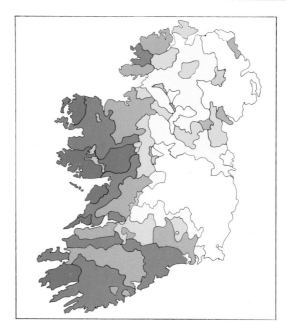

Map 7
Percentage Irish speakers 1851
  Less than 10
  10-25
  25-50
  50-80
  More than 80

10. *The Last Circuit of Pilgrims at Clonmacnoise, Co. Offaly*, a watercolour by George Petrie, was painted in about 1838, several years before the Famine struck, with devastating consequences for the poorest classes and for the Irish language

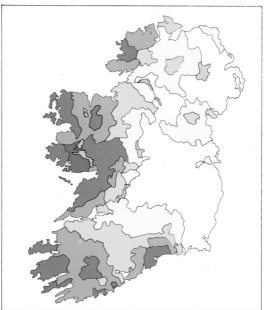

Map 8
Percentage Irish speakers 1891
  Less than 10
  10-25
  25-50
  50-80
  More than 80

11. A reconstructed *bothán scóir* or one-room cottage of landless rural families.

population was 6,552,386; this represents a net decrease of 1,622,738 between 1841 and 1851. It can be argued that the total decrease of population caused by death and emigration during the Great Famine years was in reality much greater, since the population must have continued to increase after 1841. Projections on the pre-Famine growth rate would put the total population at about 10,000,000 by 1850. Be that as it may, what cannot be doubted is that the devastation, whatever its full extent, was suffered mainly by the poorest classes. An examination by Caoimhín Ó Danachair of census statistics on types of dwellings shows that in County Limerick, for instance, there were in 1841 21,493 class 4 houses (ie one-roomed dwellings called *botháin scóir*); in 1851 there were 7,460. Since the other three classes of houses in 1851 show a total increase of 2,006 over the 1841 figure, there may have been some reclassification, and even some overall improvement in conditions, but that still leaves an unexplained disappearance of 12,027 dwellings of the poorest type. This is probably a fair measure of the disaster which the Great Famine represented for the poorest class, at least in the areas most seriously affected. This was precisely the class, in those very areas, which would still have been Irish-speaking when the Great Famine struck.

All of this is, of course, somewhat speculative. The first definitive figure for Irish speakers is that provided by the 1851 Census in which, for the first time, a question on language was included. In 1851 the number was 1,524,286; slightly less than 25% of the total population. The regional distribution of Irish speakers, as portrayed in Map 7, suggests that the language had been in decline in the east of the country long before the Famine had had its effect. An analysis by age group of the 1851 figures leads to the same conclusion:

Of those who were born between 1751 and 1761, and were still alive in 1851, 35.12% were Irish speaking. The information which this provides on the total situation in 1751-61 can only be implicit, since it is not possible to say with certainty to what

extent the loss of Irish speakers had been disproportionately greater nor what was the ratio in 1751-1761 between the percentage represented by Irish speakers in the under ten age group and the overall percentage of Irish speakers: in 1851, for example, the overall percentage of Irish speakers was twice what Irish speakers represented in the under ten age group. Despite these uncertainties it must be acknowledged that 35.12% for 1751-1761 is remarkably low and, even when allowance is made for a greater mortality in Irish-speaking classes and districts, it is difficult not to conclude that by that time those acquiring Irish as a first language were already a minority of their age group, taking Ireland as a whole.

Analysis by age group also provides an indication of the decrease that will inevitably occur in the future, as older and more Irish-speaking generations pass away. Thus, the fact that no more than 12.66% were Irish-speaking of those who were ten years or under in 1851 points to a certain further decline in overall numbers. In the event, the decrease was much greater than might have been projected from the 1851 figure because, with each passing decade, the number acquiring Irish as a first language represented an ever decreasing percentage of the age group. By 1891 only 30,785 of those under ten were Irish-speaking, compared with 166,839 in 1851; and this represented 3.5% of the age group, compared with 12.66% of the age group in 1851. The size of the traditional Irish-speaking community in the 20th century is already determined in those figures.

The retreat of Irish to discontinuous peripheral areas was inescapable although, naturally, older speakers were available throughout much of the 1891 area until the middle of the 20th century, as is shown by the distribution of locations from which it was possible, mainly in the late 1940s and 1950s, to compile information for H. Wagner's *Linguistic Atlas and Survey of Irish Dialects.*

13. Irish in the 20th century

The regions in which Irish has survived as a

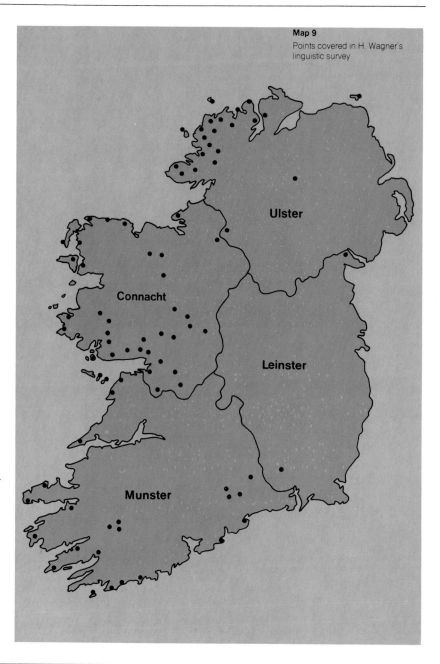

Map 9
Points covered in H. Wagner's linguistic survey

Ulster

Connacht

Leinster

Munster

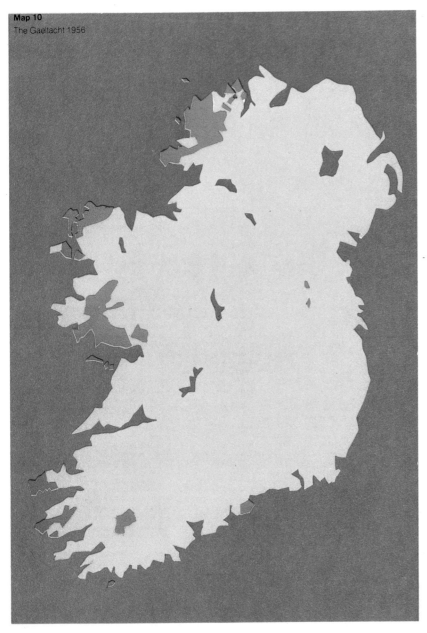

Map 10
The Gaeltacht 1956

community language are termed collectively *Gaeltacht*. Though their population has for most of the period been decreasing, the Gaeltacht areas have remained relatively stable in regard to language use during the greater part of the 20th century.

In 1971 the total population of the Gaeltacht areas was 65,982, of whom 54,940 were returned as Irish speakers, or 83.3% of the total. By 1981 the population of the Gaeltacht areas was exactly 75,000. This represents an increase of more than 9,000 over the 1971 figure, due in part to boundary changes effected in 1974, but the proportion of Irish speakers at 58,026 had by 1981 declined to 77.4% of the total. Apart from that, it is necessary to distinguish between the incidence of competence to speak the language and the incidence of actual use. It is fairly reliably estimated that no more than 25,000 of the Gaeltacht population now use Irish consistently in day-to-day communication.

The truth is that a new decline appears to have set in over the last 15 years and many Irish-speaking parents in Gaeltacht areas have been using English only with their children. In a survey recently carried out by John Harris, children in Gaeltacht primary schools reported their home language as follows:

English only	46.1%
English and Irish	33.7%
Irish only	20.2%

Of course, schools situated within the Gaeltacht may in many instances draw some of their attendance from outside of the Gaeltacht area, and this would account for some of the surprisingly high percentage of those reporting English only but, even so, the trend does seem set again for decline. This new deterioration has been brought about by a modern industrialisation programme which greatly increased the number of English-speaking situations within the Gaeltacht and gave rise to an in-migration of English-speaking families; by the effects of predominantly English-speaking modern media, especially television, on small rural communities; and by new patterns of mobility which have made journeys to English-speaking areas an everyday matter.

On the other hand, Irish is not confined to the Gaeltacht. In the 1971 Census 789,429 people, representing 28.3% of the population of the Republic of Ireland, were returned as Irish speakers.

This is the highest figure since 1881 and does reflect the deliberate efforts made by the Irish State to maintain Irish. The figures make no distinction between degrees of competence, nor degrees of use, but there are throughout the State many individuals and families whose first language is Irish. In 1971 the number of children between 3 and 9 years of age who were returned as Irish speakers was 94,481, about 21% of the age group. That that figure includes many who are regarded as knowing Irish because they are studying it at school is shown by the fact that in the 3-4 year old group the percentage of Irish speakers is 5.5%. However 5.5% is two percentage points higher than the percentage of Irish speakers in the under 10 year age group in 1891.

In 1981, according to preliminary figures, the total number returned as Irish speakers was 1,018,312, representing 31.6% of the population; the number of speakers in the 3-4 year old group had declined to 4.9% and this may be linked to the recent deterioration in the position of the language in Gaeltacht areas.

If Irish speakers are mapped on the basis of their actual numbers within an area, rather than on the basis of percentages, the regional pattern is quite different, and it demonstrates in a striking way the recent growth in the numbers of Irish speakers in urban areas where, of course, they remain a small percentage of the total population.

Again, however, this is a statement of the number of those returned as Irish speakers; it is not an indicator of levels of use.

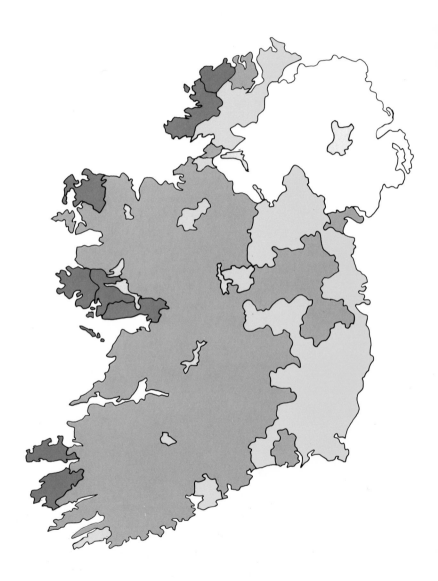

Map 11

Percentage Irish speakers 1971

Less than 10
10-25
25-50
50-80
More than 80

Map 12

Distribution of Irish speakers in 1971

Numbers per Rural District

    − 3,000
3,001 - 5,000
5,001 - 10,000
10,001 +

Next page

12. Nature study class in an Irish
speaking school in Dublin, one of a
number of new State-funded Irish
schools established outside Gaeltacht
areas.

13. A *Bord na Gaeilge* advertisement
promoting the use of Irish.

Actual use is a different variable. According to a recent survey published by the Linguistics Institute of Ireland, respondents reported the extent of their use of Irish as follows:

Domain of use of Irish	Users as percentage of total
1. in conversation since leaving school	18%
2. in writing since leaving school	5%
3. frequently or normally in home	5%
4. sometimes in home	25%
5. programme in Irish on television	72%

The discrepancy between 1 and 4 is presumably because 4 does not necessarily involve the respondent personally. It will be noted that the response to 3 accords well with the Census figure for Irish speakers in the 3-4 year age group. 5 is a passive activity and suggests a high level of passive competence in the language.

A high degree of passive knowledge is closely matched, perhaps corroborated, by the existence of a high measure of favourable attitudes towards the maintenance of Irish. The Linguistics Institute survey has revealed the following scale of support for provision for Irish use in public domains:

Provision for use	Percentage of respondents favouring
on television	76%
in Civil Service	75%
in Dáil (Parliament)	66%
in public forms, notices	70%
in tests for public servants	71%

Again, according to the same survey, the degree to which Irish is regarded by respondents as a symbol of cultural identity is compatible with their responses on public provision:

13

I t's amazing how easily things come back to you once you try them again. The flair for assembling models... the skills of a sport, perhaps... or maybe just the satisfaction of speaking your own language. As the song says: 'Let's try to make it part of every day; show the world that we can say it, our own way.' Bain triail as, mar sin, sa bhaile leis na páistí; ag obair, nó le do chairde. Just think of what it means to pass on a language of our own. And very quickly the pieces all fit together.

Bain triail as.

Our Language. It's part of what we are.

BORD NA GAEILGE

Proposition	Percentage of respondents in agreement
Without Irish, Ireland would certainly lose its identity as a separate culture	66%
It is important that children should grow up knowing Irish	69%
No real Irish person can be against the revival of Irish	73%

Modern Ireland has, accordingly, a complex linguistic profile. English is by far the dominant language. The number of monoglot Irish speakers, particularly if one excludes pre-school children in Irish-speaking households, is tiny; the exact number has, however, not been published. On the other hand, Irish is the first language of at least 100,000 people in Ireland; again, it is not possible to say how many exactly, since the Census data do not distinguish kinds of competence. The number would consist of (i) a majority of the inhabitants of the Gaeltacht areas; (ii) people from Gaeltacht areas settled in other parts of the country; (iii) others in predominantly English-speaking areas whose home language is, or was, Irish and who maintain a facility in it. Whatever their exact number, those whose everyday language is Irish are no more than a fraction of the 31.6% of the population which, in the 1981 Census, was returned as Irish-speaking. The figure 31.6% arises because some of those whose competence is passive rather than active report themselves as speakers. The reality seems to be that about 10% have a high active, i.e. speaking, competence and a relatively high pattern of use, and that a further 30%, or so, have an extensive passive competence, i.e. can understand broadcasts, announcements, public notices, and less complicated written communications; perhaps a further 20% have a limited passive competence. Apart from competence, surveys consistently show that a majority of the community recognises Irish as the ancestral language, regards it therefore as a significant part of the native cultural tradition, and supports State provision for its maintenance and promotion.

Thus, because of the surviving widespread identification with Irish, there is in Ireland a bilingual culture in which, though there is a great disparity in numbers of speakers between English and Irish, the relationship is not simply one of major language to minor language. Equally, because commitment to the use of Irish is found throughout the State, despite the special position of the Gaeltacht areas where traditional Irish has survived as the everyday language, the relationship is not that of national language to regional language either; the pattern of language use does not follow a territorial imperative by which it is appropriate to use one language in one region but not in another, nor are distinctive subcommunities as strongly defined by language allegiance as they are, for example, by denominational allegiance.

This curious pattern of language, in which the survival of Irish is to a large extent dependent on a conscious sense of historical continuity, may now be increasingly vulnerable because of the political and social stresses which Ireland has been undergoing during the last fifteen years. The pattern has had its origin, not only in the folk memory which exists because the decline of Irish has been so recent and so abrupt but also in the relatively successful restoration of Irish by an independent Irish State to crucial public domains such as education and public administration. Whatever the future holds, it cannot be doubted that the effectiveness of the State's language policy, now urgently needing revision, will be critical.

14. The Restoration of Irish
The beginning of the restoration of status to the Irish language can be traced to the late 18th century. It is marked specifically by the publication in 1789 of Charlotte Brooke's *Reliques of Irish Poetry,* the first anthology of secular literature in Irish to appear in print. The book is evidence of an awakening academic interest in Irish language

14. The great majority of placenames in Ireland derive from the Irish language. Modern roadsigns show both the original and the anglicised forms. In some cases Irish and English forms are of different origin, e.g. Dublin and *Ath Cliath.*

15. Headquarters of *Udarás na Gaeltachta,* the Gaeltacht authority

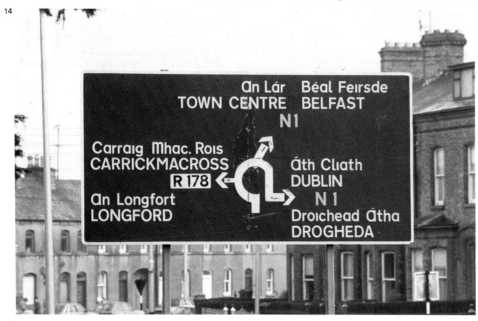

15

and literature on the part of the English-speaking ascendancy. The interest gradually grew. One of Charlotte Brooke's assistants Theophilus Ó Flannagáin, founded the Gaelic Society in 1807. It was not to survive for long, but it was succeeded by similar societies such as the Archaelogian Society and the Iberno-Celtic Society. These societies were in the main motivated by an interest in antiquities and literature and drew at least some of their inspiration from the Romantic movement. Their importance was that they began the publication and dissemination of literature in Irish and recovered some intellectual respectability for Irish studies. One of the more successful of such typically 19th century societies was the Ossianic Society which published some excellent editions of Irish texts such as Standish Hayes-O'Grady's *Tóruigheacht Dhiarmada Uí Dhuibhne agus Ghráinne* and John O'Daly's *Laoithe Fiannuigheachta*. It was founded in 1853 'for the Preservation and Publication of MSS in the Irish Language, illustrative of the Fenian period of Irish History'.

As the century passed and the accelerating decline of Irish as a community language became evident, literary interests were augmented by a growing concern for the preservation of the spoken language as a precious heritage. Societies which had primarily language maintenance objectives began to be formed. The Society for the Preservation of the Irish Language which was founded in 1876 included in its membership people who had earlier been members of the Ossianic Society. However, old attitudes die hard, and in 1878 those who desired a more radical policy for the support of the spoken language broke away and formed the Gaelic Union. In 1882 the Gaelic Union began the publication of *Irisleabhar na Gaedhilge,* a journal which for a generation was to be a major influence in redeveloping Irish as a literary medium and in promoting a language revival philosophy. Such efforts reached their culmination in 1893 when the Gaelic League *(Conradh na Gaeilge)* was founded by Douglas Hyde, Eoin Mac Néill, Eugene O'Growney, and others. The League took up with

greater vigour the revivalist aspects of the work of the Gaelic Union. As a direct consequence of its teaching, when the Irish Free State was established in 1922, Irish was designated the 'national language' and competence in it became compulsory for entry to the civil service, police, and army. It was given a central place in the primary school curriculum, and was universally introduced into the secondary school system where, however, it had had a secure place since 1913 when it became compulsory for matriculation to the National University. In the 1937 Constitution, which is still in force, the status of Irish is reaffirmed. The relevant clause in Article 8 is:
'The Irish language as the national language is the first official language.'

In addition to establishing its official status and promoting it in education and the public services, the Irish State has made various other provisions for the maintenance of the Irish language: in 1943 *Comhdháil Náisiúnta na Gaeilge* ('Irish language national assembly') was given funds as a coordinating agency for voluntary language organisations; *Bord na Leabhar Gaeilge* was established in 1952 to supervise the allocation of subsidies for the publication of books in Irish; a State Department of the Gaeltacht was established in 1956; *Gaeltarra Éireann* ('Gael-products') began in 1957 as a semi-State industrial development agency for the Gaeltacht regions; in 1978, in response to Gaeltacht protest activity, it was replaced by *Udarás na Gaeltachta* ('The Gaeltacht Authority'), which has essentially the same functions as *Gaeltarra,* but some of whose members are elected from the Gaeltacht regions by popular vote; *Raidió na Gaeltachta,* an Irish language radio station, serving especially the Gaeltacht regions, again in response to popular demand, began broadcasting in 1972; *Bord na Gaeilge,* which had begun tentatively in 1975, was in 1978 established by Act of the *Oireachtas* (Legislature) as the official State agency for planning and policy-making in relation to the Irish language.

On Ireland's joining the European Communities in 1973, Irish became an official, though not a working, language of the EEC. As a consequence, in 1973 the texts of the treaties establishing the European Communities were published in Irish. In Séamas Daltún's translation, the language copes effectively and lucidly enough with that special idiom. For example:
Measúnófar na tobhaigh, go bliantúil, ar na táirgí éagsúla de réir a meánluacha, gan a ráta a dhul thar a 1 faoin gcéad mura mbeidh sin údaraithe roimh ré ag an gComhairle, ag gníomhú di trí thromlach dhá thrian.

'The levies shall be assessed annually on the various products according to their average value; the rate thereof shall not, however, exceed 1 per cent unless previously authorised by the Council, acting by a two-thirds majority'. Well at least it probably proves that the ancient tongue has not entirely lost its resilience.

16. A page from the Book of Armagh ▷ which was completed in 807 A.D. by Ferdomnach, Abbot of Armagh. The Book of Armagh is the earliest manuscript preserved in Ireland in which there is contemporary text in Irish. The script is an example of Irish minuscule script which, with little change or modification continued until the 20th century as the form in which Irish was normally written.

16

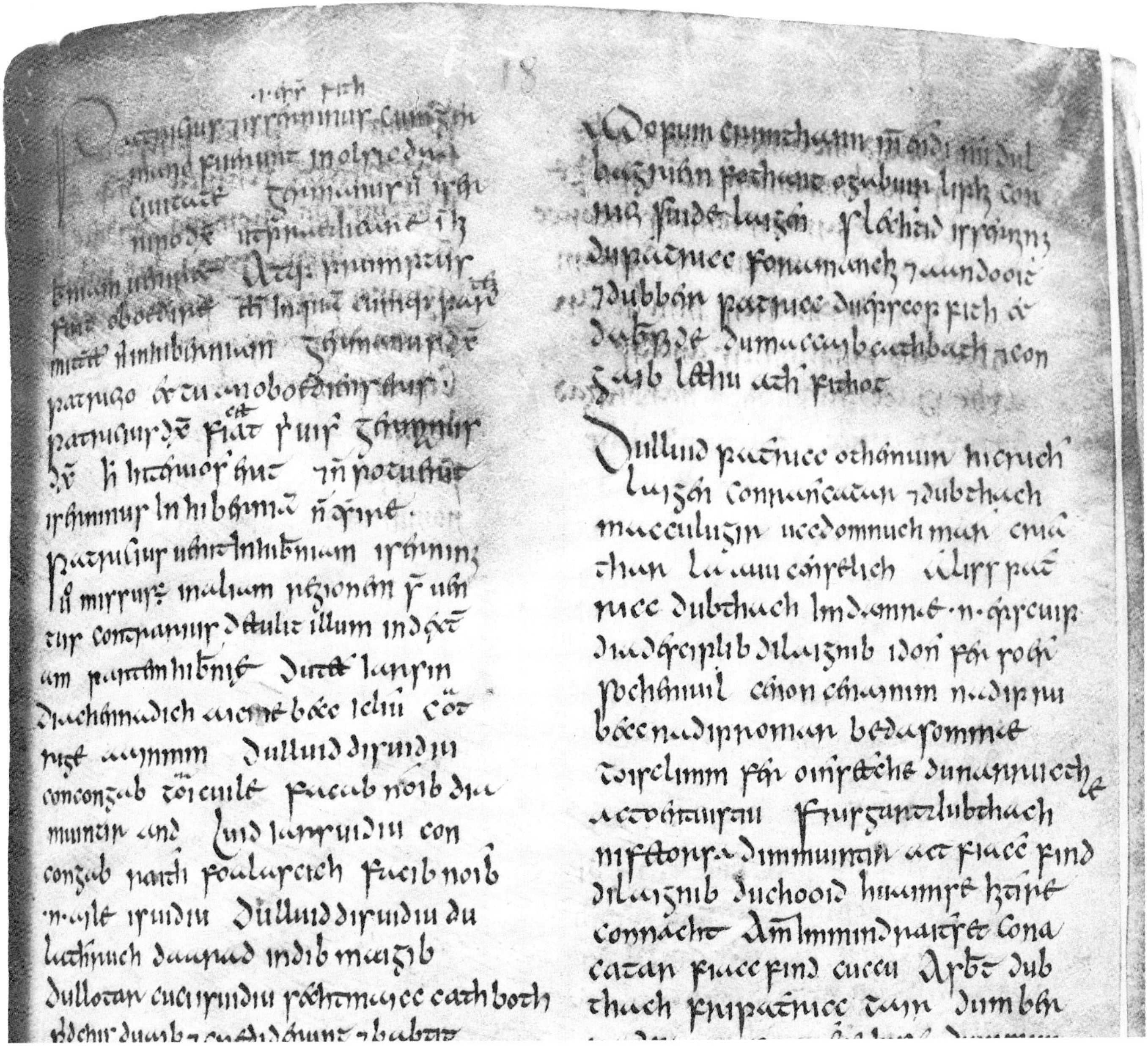

1. Primitive Irish and Old Irish

The earliest form of Irish now known is that which has been preserved in ogham inscriptions. The linguistic information obtainable from these inscriptions is, however, limited. Their purpose was to commemorate or proclaim individuals, whose names appear in the genitive inflection denoting '(in memory) of x' or '(monument) of x'. The convention required nothing more but, in any case, the constraints of the medium, which necessitated writing along the edge of the stone, placed physical limitations on the length of the text.

A fairly typical example from west Kerry is:
Cunamaqqi Avi Corbbi
which may be normalised as:
Cunamaqqi Avii Corbi
and means 'of Cunamaqqos grandson of Corbos'. Though inscriptions might occasionally be a good deal longer than this, their content always remains essentially the same, e.g. from north Kerry:

Coillabbotas Maqi Corbbi Maqi Mocoi Qerai
'of Coillabus son of Corbos son of one of the people of Qeraios'. Apart from personal names, therefore, and the small set of words used in name formation, such as *maqqos* 'son', *avios* 'grandson', very few items of vocabulary have survived in ogham. The most significant are, perhaps: *inigena* 'daughter', *néta(s)* 'of champion', *velitas* 'of poet'.

Although the material is thus restricted, it is not without value as an exemplification of some of the grammatical and phonetic features of a very early variety of Irish. This very early Irish is significantly different from the form of *Old Irish* recorded in the glosses (see Part I) of the 8th and 9th centuries, in distinction to which it is sometimes termed *Primitive Irish*.

In Primitive Irish, words are longer and have more archaic inflectional endings than they do in the language of the glosses. The distance between the two forms of language is almost exactly comparable to the distance between the language of the glosses and Gaulish, as the following tables of comparison show:

Gaulish	8th Century Irish	
nertomáros	nertmar	'powerful'
senobena	senben	'old woman'
vindomagos	findmag	'fair plain'

Ogham Irish	8th Century Irish	
Catubutas	Cathbad	'of Catubus/ Cathub'
inigena	ingen	'daughter'
velitas	filed	'of poet'

Similarly, the name *Cunamaqqi Avii Corbi* would by the 8th century have the form *Conmaicc Áui Chuirb.* Both name and cognomen occur in the later form in the genealogies recorded in the 12th century *Book of Leinster,* though this actual combination does not.

For Primitive Irish *Cunamaqqi Avii Corbi* to evolve to the later *Conmaicc Aui Chuirb,* considerable linguistic change had to occur (see Table 4) and, though languages may change more rapidly at some periods than at others, it seems more than might be expected for a period of approximately three hundred years, if the traditional dates for ogham and the Old Irish glosses are accepted. Part of the explanation must be that, although extant writings in it are exasperatingly meagre, Primitive Irish was a conservative literary norm which, while it does show evolution during its productive period, lagged behind the changes which were occuring in the vernacular language by a considerable time. It would consequently also appear that the first Christian scholars adopted a more colloquial norm for the new literary tradition which they established. That they should have done so was consistent with their revisionary attitude to all aspects of the old pagan tradition, and the transition to the new convention must have been abrupt. It was, nevertheless, firmly controlled because in the language of the glosses there is a clearly defined and highly stable norm with no evidence of experimentation, nor any significant reflection of dialect variation. As David

Table 4

Stages in the evolution from Ogham Irish to Old Irish as exemplified by Cunamaqqi Avii Corbi

Cunamaqqi Avii Corbi

1. (a) is modified by consonant softening *(lenition)* i.e. single consonants between vowels change from stops to fricatives e.g. *c* to *ch*, *m* to *v* though the later spelling will not show it
∴ * Cunaμaqqi Avii Chorbi

(b) is modified by *vowel affection* i.e. *u* changes to *o* when the following syllable has *a, o* changes to *u* when the following syllable has *i*
∴ * Conaμaqqi Avii Churbi

(c) is modified by change of *q* to *k,* written *c*
∴ * Conaμacci Avii Churbi

(d) is modified by *palatalisation,* i.e. consonants develop a distinctive slender pronunciation before *-i*
∴ * Conaμaĺcci Avii Chuĺrbi

(e) is modified by change of *av* to *au* before a vowel
∴ * Conaμaĺcci auii Chuĺrbi

2. is modified by *apocope* i.e. open syllables at the end of words are elided
∴ * Conaμaĺcc Aui Chuĺrb

3. is modified by *syncope* i.e. syllables in the middle of words are elided
∴ * Conμaĺcc Aui Chuĺrb

Which, in the spelling convention of the glosses, is represented as:
Conmaicc Áui Chuirb

Next page
17. A passage from a 9th century Irish copy of the 6th century grammatical treatise of Priscian, with annotations or glosses in Irish.

18. The first page of the legal text *Bretha Im Fuillema Gell* ('Judgements on Pledge Interests'), an early 8th century text preserved in a 14th century compilation of legal texts.

Greene so aptly put it, 'it was not so much a revolution as a constitutional reform'.

Thus, the language itself provides evidence that there was a linguistic 'constitution' which was sustained because the early Christian scholars inherited a mature literary tradition, in which at least some of their members must have been educated participants. It was, it is true, a largely oral tradition but this is in no way incompatible with the existence of a well-defined norm which embraced variation along a stylistic scale from conservative to colloquial.

2. Varieties of Old Irish

In Ireland very little writing in Irish has been preserved in manuscripts which are earlier than the late 11th century. An extensive corpus of material has, however, been transmitted in manuscripts dating from the 12th century and after and, with the language of the glosses providing a fairly precisely datable linguistic criterion, it is now accepted among scholars of the early language that many texts, although known only from later manuscripts, are substantially older than even the glosses.

Much further study of extant records is required to determine more precisely the dating of Old Irish texts. The task is complicated, not only by the fact that many texts are preserved in late manuscripts with many corruptions in transmission, but by the fact that any individual text may be archaising or innovatory in relation to its own time. It had for long been a common view, for example, that passages in the alliterative style called *rosc* represented an archaic stratum which had been subsumed from earlier sources into later versions of texts. Recently, however, one of the younger generation of Irish scholars, Liam Breatnach, has conclusively demonstrated that a *rosc* passage in the legal text *Bretha Nemed* betrays Christian influences and was, in fact, composed between 721 and 742 by a member of the Munster learned family of Ó Búirecháin. The arcane *Bretha Nemed* text, *rosc* included, is therefore contemporary with the language of the glosses and must be seen as deliberately archaising rather than actually archaic. The systematic research which has brought this difficult text into such clear perspective will eventually, it may be hoped, lead to an accurate chronological and stylistic classification of most extant early writings in Irish.

In the meantime, it is safe to conclude that, along a gradually changing cline, it is useful to distinguish *Early Old Irish* from *Classical Old Irish.* However, as they are the medium of a complex literary and learned tradition, they cannot be regarded as standing in linear chronological sequence; they can, at least for some of the overall period, alternate stylistically. Not only are there no abrupt transitions from one variety to the other but, as with the transition from Primitive Irish to Old Irish, there is some overlap between the two in real time. In general, though, Classical Old Irish may be associated with the 8th and 9th centuries, Early Old Irish with the late 6th and 7th centuries. Classical Old Irish is the language of most of the glosses, of a substantial body of lyric poetry, of the earliest near-complete version of the epic *Táin Bó Cúailgne;* it is the subject of R. Thurneysen's classic description, *A Grammar of Old Irish.* A definitive account of the characteristics of Early Old Irish, or an agreed catalogue of its literature, does not yet exist.

3. Middle Irish

The period of Classical Old Irish was coming to an end before the 9th century drew to a close. There followed a period of about two hundred and fifty years from which surviving texts are characterised by the appearance of many innovatory grammatical forms intermingled with correct Old Irish usage and obvious attempts at archaism. This is the period of *Middle Irish* (see Table 5). It is a period of confusion and uncertainty in which new formations intermingle randomly with the older. Nevertheless, the written language gives no hint of the regional diversity which must have existed in the spoken language. While the period may be marked by a certain pedantry and literary conservatism, as the learned struggled to adhere to an increasingly remote norm, it was not a period in which the learned classes' control of education and the written form was breaking down.

Table 5

Some innovations which mark the transition from Old Irish to Middle Irish

(i)

the simplification of noun inflections as exemplified by the noun *céle* 'companion':

	Old Irish	Middle Irish
Nominative	céle	céle
Genitive	céli	céle
Dative	céliu	céle

This simplification is a consequence of the reduction of short vowel contrasts in weakly stressed syllables.

(ii)

the simplification of verbal inflections as exemplified by the simple verb *beirid* 'bears' and the compound verb *do-airbir* 'grants'.

In the Old Irish system the independent form of the simple verb was *beirid* and the dependent form, i.e. the form used with prefixes, was *-beir*. Thus, *beirid* 'bears', *ní beir* 'does not bear'. Since the compound, by definition, involved prefixes its independent form was *do-airbir*, without the ending *-id*, but its dependent form was marked by a stress shift; thus *ní tairbir*. By the Middle Irish period this complexity was being greatly simplified:

Old Irish	Middle Irish
beirid, -beir	beirid, -beir
do-airbir,	tairbirid,
-tairbir	-tairbir

(iii)

independent forms of personal pronouns began to be used as the subject of copula constructions and as the object of transitive verbs:

Old Irish	Middle Irish	
am mac	is mac mé	'I am a son'
ro-m-chráid	ro-chráid mé	'he has harassed me'

4. Varieties of Early Modern Irish

From the end of the 12th century the second great norm in the history of the Irish language had begun to emerge. It is the norm particularly associated with the secular schools of language and literature which were conducted in the period 1200-1600 by a professional class of literary scholars called *filidh* (singular *file*), or collectively *aos dána*. It is the variety of Irish now generally known as *Early Modern Irish* or *Classical Modern Irish* (see Table 6).

Table 6
Some innovations which mark the transition from Middle Irish to Early Modern Irish

(i)
various verbal prefixes are assimilated to *do* —

Middle Irish	Early Modern Irish	
do-bheir	do-bheir	'gives'
ad-chí	do-chí	'sees'
no-léigeadh	do-léigeadh	'used allow'
ro-ghabh	do-ghabh	'took'

(ii)
independent personal pronouns began, optionally, to function as the subject of verbs:

Middle Irish	Early Modern Irish	
atú	atá mé	'I am'
ataoi	atá tú	'you (sg.) are'
atá	atá sé, sí	'he, she, it, is'
atám	atá sinn	'we are'
atáithí	atá sibh	'you are'
atáid	atá siad	'they are'

As in earlier periods of the language, newer formations may mix apparently indiscriminately with the old. Thus the poet Gofraidh Fionn O Dálaigh who died in 1387 writes:
mar tú dá bhás ní bhiadh mé . . .
'as I am because of his death I would not be . . .'
where within a single line of verse *tú* is the older inflected 1st person, 'I am', but *bhiadh mé* 'I would be' shows the independent pronoun formation.

In this variable system which constitutes Early Modern Irish three broad stylistic tendencies are distinguishable:

(i) a mainstream literary usage sometimes called *ceart na bhfileadh* 'the poets' standard' but referred to simply as *ceart* in what have survived of the poets' grammatical treatises; it is marked, for example, by more elaborate noun inflections and by less fused forms of certain phrases (see Table 7);

(ii) a somewhat more casual usage called *canamhain* 'speech, speaking' in the grammatical treatises; it was probably quite close to some spoken variety — perhaps the speech of the educated classes — but it nevertheless reflects a clear concept of correctness and firmly excludes many forms which must have been well established in the speech of the ordinary people;

Table 7
Examples of *Ceart* compared with *Canamhain*

(i)

don ghiol dhonn	don gheal dhonn

The difference is in *ghiol~ gheal; ghiol* is a special dative inflection which is discarded without loss of meaning in *canamhain;* with or without the special dative inflection, the phrase means 'for the noble fair one' — a rather unnatural phrase, composed for the sake of grammatical illustration.

(ii)

gus an dtráth-sa	*gusdrásda*

Canamhain has a fused, obviously casual, form; *ceart* has a typically careful form, preserving the integrity of the elements of the phrase, which means 'to this time, hitherto'.

(iii) an archaising style, as a mark presumably of learning and authority, used primarily in historical and pseudo-historical writings; a notorious example is Lughaidh Ó Cléirigh's biography of Aodh Ruadh O Domhnaill, Lord of Tír Chonaill: *Beatha Aodha Ruaidh;* though written in the early 17th century, it consistently adheres to 12th century grammatical usage (see table 8).

Table 8
Analysis of a sentence from *Beatha Aodha Ruaidh*
Ba hann do-rala do ghoibhernóir Chóigidh
Chonnacht a bheith an adhaigh sin ar an gcnuc hi
gcomhfhochraibh Tuillsce.
'The fact was that the governor of the Province of
Connacht happened that night to be on the hill
near Tulsk.'

Ba hann
literally 'it was in it' i.e. 'it was a fact that'; the use of
a past tense form of the copule *ba,* rather than the
present tense form *is,* is by now somewhat
pedantic in this kind of construction.

do-rala
an old independent verbal form which had been
replaced by *tarla* (see Table 5 (ii)) before the Early
Modern period.

goibhernóir
. mutated to *ghoibhernóir* after the preposition *do,*
is a contemporary borrowing; though the
archaising style was marked by the use of
obsolete words and phrases, new lexical items
were not avoided.

an adhaigh sin
'that night'; *adhaigh* 'night' is an old nominative
case which had long been superseded by
oidhche, in origin a genitive/dative inflection of the
word.

ar an gcnuc
'on the hill' has the *ceart na bhfileadh* dative
inflection of *cnoc* 'hill', but the mutation in this
context should be *ch-* not *gc-;* this may be due to
scribal error.

i gcomhfhochraibh
'in environs (of)' is a rather stilted expression,
typical of the style.

The professional literary men of the period have
traditionally been associated with an archaising
and obscure style and were alleged by 16th
century English commentators to be widely
incomprehensible. The Oxford scholar Edmund
Campion in 1571 wrote: 'But the true Irish indeede
differeth somuch from that they commonly
speake, that scarce one among five score, can
either write, read, or understand it. Therefore it is
prescribed among certaine their Poets, and other
Students of Antiquitie'. By 'true Irish' Campion, in
accordance with the linguistic views of his time,
would have meant that which was believed to be
historically correct. He may well have received his
information from contemporary Irish informants,
as the belief that the poets' language was
incomprehensible is corroborated by Irish tradition
itself. For example, in the 13th century text,
Tromdhámh Ghuaire, which satirises the poet
class for their arrogant behaviour, when the chief
poet Dallán has recited a poem of numbing
triteness in obscure language, the king Aodh is
made to say:
is maith an duan gibé do thuigfeadh í
'the poem is good, whoever might understand it'.
Later, when Dallán has recited a lampoon against
him, Aodh's comment is:
is cubhas dúinne nach feadamarne an fearr nó an
measa sin iná an chéad-duan do-rinnis
'we confess that we do not know whether that is
better or worse than the first poem which you
made'.

This portrayal of the poets' compositions no doubt
had some basis in reality; some poets were rather
bad at their craft and took refuge in a largely
meaningless pedantry. In the main, though, the
poets were quite up to date in their grammar and
modernising in their vocabulary. Despite the
constraints of very strict and complex metrical
rules, the best of them achieved an easy style, as a
random stanza from an address by Gofraidh
Fionn Ó Dálaigh to the Earl of Desmond will
illustrate:

Dá dteagmhainn duid ar druim róid
seocham do ghéabhtha, a Ghearóid,
gan mé ná thú rinn do rádh
agus rinn chlú ar mo chomhrádh.
'If I should meet you in the middle of the road you would go past me, Gearóid, without saying me or thee to us, though my conversation is in high regard'. This must be a fairly close representation of a contemporary conversational style and, in fact, may be judged closer to the modern spoken language than is, for example, the language of Chaucer to Modern English.

Although a great corpus of writing in diverse styles has survived from the period of Early Modern Irish, it provides little tangible information on regional or social differences in speech, though both kinds of variation must have existed. Many texts contain dialogue which, with a minimum of grammatical modification, would be entirely authentic as representations of present day speech, and yet it gives no hint of region, nor any mark of social status that can now be recognised. For example, in a 13th century Irish version of the Odyssey, there is the following conversation between Penelope and Ulysses:
P. *A dhaoine maithe, cársa cia sibhse eidir?*
   'Good people, who are you at all?'
U. *Uilix Mac Leirtis mise*
   'I am Uilix Mac Leirtis'
P. *Ní tú an tUilix rob aithnidh dúinne*
   'You are not the Uilix who was known to us'
U. *Is mé go deimhin agus innéasad mo chomhartha duit.*
   'I am indeed and I shall tell you my sign'
P. *Caidhe do dhealbh agus do mhuintear mása tú Uilix?*
   'What has become of your handsome appearance and your followers if you are Uilix?'
U. *Do-chuadar amugha*
   'They have gone missing'

In the Irish version, this is a respectable attempt at natural dialogue, yet the language does not depart from the literary standard. Of course, the personae represented here are aristocrats who, even in conversation, might be expected to use a form of language which had a close affinity to mainstream literary usage.

The representation of peasant speech, no matter how authentic the dialogue appears, is equally unrevealing of regional or social dialect. In the 12th century text, *Buile Shuibhne* ('Suibhne's Madness'), dialogue is put into the mouths of Abbot Mo-Ling's servants. It has a very natural ring, as when Mo-Ling's swineherd is addressed by his sister:
Atá do bhean insan fhál soin thoir ag fear oile, a mheathaigh mhiodhlaochdha
'Your wife is east in that hedge with another man, you craven coward'. So far as one can now determine, there is no attempt here either to represent the kind of local speech which swineherds or their sisters in the 12th century must have spoken, but it is probably anachronistic to expect that a medieval literary caste should possess that kind of social awareness, or have anything other than disdain for the speech of the lower orders.

In sum, Early Modern Irish, despite the stylistic variety in which we know it, is a strictly controlled literary language, autonomous of contemporary varieties of the spoken language. It was, nonetheless, a literary language which was not insensitive to the changes which were taking place in the spoken language, as its *canamhain* mode in particular demonstrates.

5. Varieties of Modern Irish
The transition from the Early Modern literary language to later literary usage occurred in particularly turbulent circumstances and continuity might well have been lost. The upheavals of the late 16th and 17th centuries swept aside the native aristocracy and professional literary class who up to then had maintained the gradually evolving literary norm. Consequently, from the 17th century on writers, being no longer part of a non-regional class, became more regional in experience and education and increasingly reflected the characteristics of their region's dialect in their

writing. As a result the written language, for the first time in its long history, became regionally diversified and autonomous traditions of Scots Gaelic, Manx, and Modern Irish began to emerge.

Regionalisms are revealed by lapses of spelling, the use of local forms which would not have been approved by the upholders of the classical norm, and in verse by sound correspondences which unambiguously reflect a local pronunciation. To confine the matter to spelling, an example from an 18th century text written by a County Cork monk, Tadhg Ó Conaill, will suffice as illustration. In his text, 2nd person plural forms of the imperative spelled as *creidig* 'believe you' or *labhraig* 'speak you' unequivocally reveal a west Munster pronunciation of the inflection as *-ig,* though the traditional spelling also occurs as in *abraidh* 'say you'. Over the whole text there are sufficient deviations from the old norm to provide fairly detailed information on the grammar and pronunciation of the writer's south Cork dialect. Tadhg Ó Conaill's writing does not differ extensively in form or style from similar texts written in the Early Modern period but the remarkable fact is that regional traits, of the kind portrayed by it, are absent almost entirely from the earlier texts and only gradually make their appearance after the collapse of the old regime.

At the end of the 19th century, when the Irish revival was gathering momentum, little was known of writers such as the 18th century Tadhg Ó Conaill who, whatever of their regionalism, wrote in Modern Irish. The texts which happened fortuitously to be available as literary models were closer to the Early Modern norm. They included especially works by the great early 17th century author Séathrún Céitinn (Geoffrey Keating). Céitinn's religious treatise *Trí Biorghaoithe an Bháis* had been published in 1890; *An Díonbhrollach,* his spirited introduction to his history *Forus Feasa ar Éirinn,* was published in 1898; and the Irish Texts Society's four-volume edition of *Forus Feasa ar Éirinn* began to appear in 1902. Such was the influence of these texts that many of those who led the literary revival

attempted to imitate the language and style of Séathrún Céitinn and argued that this was the most effective and logical way of re-establishing Irish as a literary medium. 'Keating's Irish' was, however, rejected as a model by the victorious 'speech of the people' faction led by Peadar Ó Laoghaire who for more than twenty crucial years until his death in 1920 dominated thinking on Irish grammar and usage. The result was that written Irish became more closely than ever patterned on the spoken language and consequently, also, reflected much of its regional diversity.

As Irish developed as a school subject and was increasingly used in official documents, the new diversity in the written form of the language caused major difficulties and the need for a prescriptive norm was gradually accepted. After much argument and debate, guidelines were eventually published in 1958 in the official handbook, *Gramadach na Gaeilge — An Caighdeán Oifigiúil.* Since then its recommendations have been widely adopted, universally so in official publications.

The main feature of the new norm is the abandonment of inflected forms of the verb where it is possible to use independent pronouns instead e.g. *dhíol mé* 'I sold', *dhíol tú* 'you sold' rather than *dhíolas, dhíolais* etc., and as far as possible the abandonment of redundant case inflections in nouns e.g. *an bhróg* 'the shoe', *ar an mbróg* 'on the shoe', rather than *ar an mbróig* with a special dative case inflection. The new norm is not without a certain conservatism which perhaps unconsciously reflects vestiges of the influence of *ceart na bhfileadh.* For example, it does not recognise the form *muid* as 1st person plural independent pronoun 'we, us' as in *bhí muid* 'we were', *bhuail sé muid* 'he struck us'. One suspects that this is because *muid* has no authority in the literary tradition. On the contrary, it smacks of illiteracy in that historically it has developed from a 1st person plural inflectional ending which, as the verb + independent pronoun pattern became predominant, was detached and treated as a free

1st person plural pronoun, in time to replace in all grammatical contexts the older independent form *sinn* in most areas where the 1st plural independent pronoun is now used with verbs. The new norm avoided giving recognition to this development.

Since, prior to the 17th century, documentary evidence of regional variation in the language was slight, the impression is easily obtained that the emergence of dialect is a recent phenomenon. Sometimes this is implied in the work of Irish linguists. For example, D. A. Binchy, editor of *Corpus Iuris Hibernici,* in a discussion of the later law texts has written 'that on rare occasions they supply evidence of emerging dialect differences'. Now, in principle, once a language has for some generations been spoken over a wide area by physically separate communities, regional variation can be expected in it. Regional variation must, therefore, have been well established by the Old Irish period. This does not, of course, mean that regional dialects once in existence must inevitably continue to diverge. Divergence would constantly be modified to the extent that there was cultural and social cohesion between the communities: the requirements of mobility and wider communication, and adherence to shared norms would tend to disseminate change so that at any given period a degree of unity is maintained. Older divergences would, therefore, constantly be eliminated. The oldest divergence which still exists is the survival in the spoken language in Scotland, and now in literary Scots Gaelic, of bisyllabic forms which have long been monosyllabic in Ireland. For example, Old Irish *laa* 'day' was a bisyllable and still is in Scotland; in Modern Irish it is pronounced and written as a long monosyllable *lá.* Old bisyllables such as *laa, lá* have been treated as long monosyllables in the literary tradition since the Middle Irish period and the divergence may have occurred in the spoken tradition even before the end of the Old Irish period.

Contemporary forms of the spoken language are, of course, fully open to inspection. In Ireland it is conventional to distinguish three main dialects: the dialect of Munster, the dialect of Connacht, and the dialect of Ulster (see Map 9). These are convenient labels but, as is normal in patterns of regional variation, the regions defined by any one feature of variation may be quite different from those defined by another, and the provincial boundaries seldom correspond exactly to the linguistic boundaries.

The following maps (13, 14, 15) illustrate some typical patterns and expressions of dialect variation in Modern Irish.

Variants of spoken Irish can only be thoroughly studied in areas where the language has survived, or at least has done so until recently. For other areas, the only sources of information are such late and localised texts as exist and the forms of

Map 13
Pronunciations of am 'time'
■ short a
▲ long a
● diphthong

Map 13 shows the pattern of variation which has resulted from a divergent treatment of a before a long nasal, m. The north is more conservative in regard to this feature and retains a without change; the area defined by this variant includes all of Ulster and the greater part of Connacht. A central variety is marked by lengthening of a; the area defined by this variant in surviving dialects is quite restricted. In the south, the vowel is pronounced as a diphthong (to rhyme with German baum); the area defined by this variant includes all of the surviving dialects of Munster. Thus, while there are three variants, only one approximates in its distribution to the provincial area; one is quite limited in distribution; and one includes most of the surviving dialects in Connacht and Ulster.

Map 14
Expressions of 'I sold'
■ do dhiolas
▲ dhiolas
● dhiol mé

Map 14 shows the regional distribution of inflected and analytical forms of the past tense of the verb with 1st person singular. There are three variants: do dhiolas 'I sold', the most conservative form, inflected for person and with the past tense prefix do; dhiolas the inflected form without the prefix, but with lenition as a vestige; dhiol mé the analytical form with independent pronoun, and again showing only lenition as a vestige of the prefix. The Early Modern norm would have allowed do dhiolas or do dhiol mé; it did not acknowledge reduction of the prefix. The area defined by the inflected form is limited to the south-west of Munster; some surviving dialects within this area are more innovating in having reduction of the prefix. The vast majority of surviving dialects have dhiol mé. The distribution pattern shows no approximation to provincial divisions.

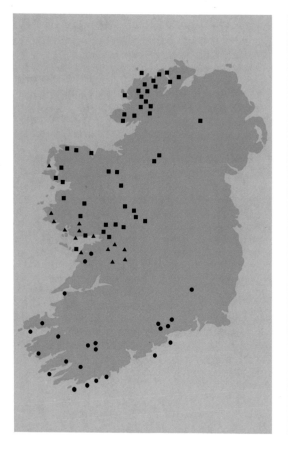

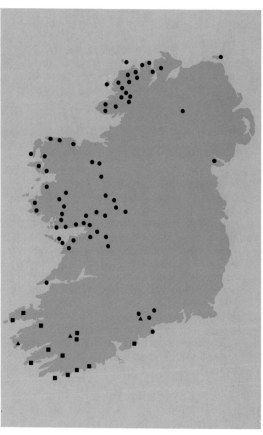

Map 15

Distribution of words for 'table'

■ bord
▲ clár
● tábla

Just as regional variation provides evidence of divergences in the spread of phonetic and grammatical change, it also shows the differing degrees to which new items of vocabulary have penetrated a language area. Map 14 shows the distribution in surviving spoken forms of Modern Irish of different words for 'table':

clár is the oldest word, being an item of Indo-European vocabulary in Irish; it is still universally used in the basic sense of 'plank of wood', 'flat surface'; it also in the Old Irish period acquired a secondary meaning, 'index, programme, register', as a translation of Latin *tabula,* and it is still universally used in that sense; as the normal term for 'table' it is found only in relic areas in the south;

bord is an early borrowing from Anglo-Saxon which probably entered Irish during the period of settlement in Britain; it is by far the most common word for 'table' in all surviving forms of the spoken language in Ireland and Scotland; in the secondary meaning of 'governing committee', which has existed in Irish since at least the 18th century, it is in universal use;

tábla, to judge from its form, entered Irish from Norman French or Early Modern English, though there would seem to be no instance of its use in surviving documents from the Early Modern period in Irish; so far as can be determined from surviving dialects, its area of distribution corresponds fairly closely to the province of Ulster; it is not now clear what circumstances led to the adoption and dissemination of *tábla* in that area; in the secondary meaning of 'table' in mathematics, statistics etc., it is the word universally used.

placenames. For many areas in which Irish was less recently in use, information on the spoken variant is therefore slight. So far as one can tell, however, there was no abrupt division between Ireland and Scotland in the forms of ordinary speech. There was instead a *dialect continuum* in which areas near one another were more similar in speech and areas which were far apart were more dissimilar. Thus, while the traditional Gaelic area remained intact, there was no point along a line from Berehaven in the south-west of Ireland to Thurso in the north of Scotland at which one would clearly cross from one language area into another.

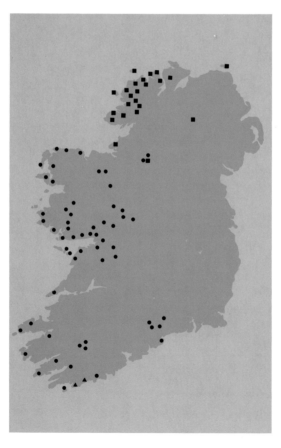

6. Emergence of an autonomous Scots Gaelic

In Gaelic Scotland, as in Ireland, the native aristocracy had given patronage to learning and shared in the uniform upper-class culture found throughout the Gaelic world. There were learned families of great prestige there and, though in its Highland retreat after the 14th century Gaelic culture in Scotland tended towards a greater conservatism, it could sometimes still take the initiative: John Carswell's translation of the liturgy of John Knox, written in the Early Modern standard and published in Edinburgh in 1567, was the first appearance of the language in print. Yet from the end of the 16th century there was an increasing atrophy of the old cultural and literary institutions. Unlike Ireland, this was not because the old social order had been overthrown; in Gaelic Scotland this did not occur until after the 1745 rebellion. It appears rather that, because the traditional cultural cohesion between Ireland and Gaelic Scotland was disrupted by political and religious upheaval, innovation on a regional basis became more natural. Without the overall cohesion to constrain divergence, local speech began to appear in literary usage.

By the end of the 17th century a distinctly Scottish literary language had been established. It has, because of the influence of the Bible in what is predominantly a reformed community, been more stable as a norm than any variety of Modern Irish until recent times. While, as in Ireland, there is no spoken norm, the speech of the highly uniform Hebrides is predominant in broadcasting, the Church and education, and comes close to serving as such.

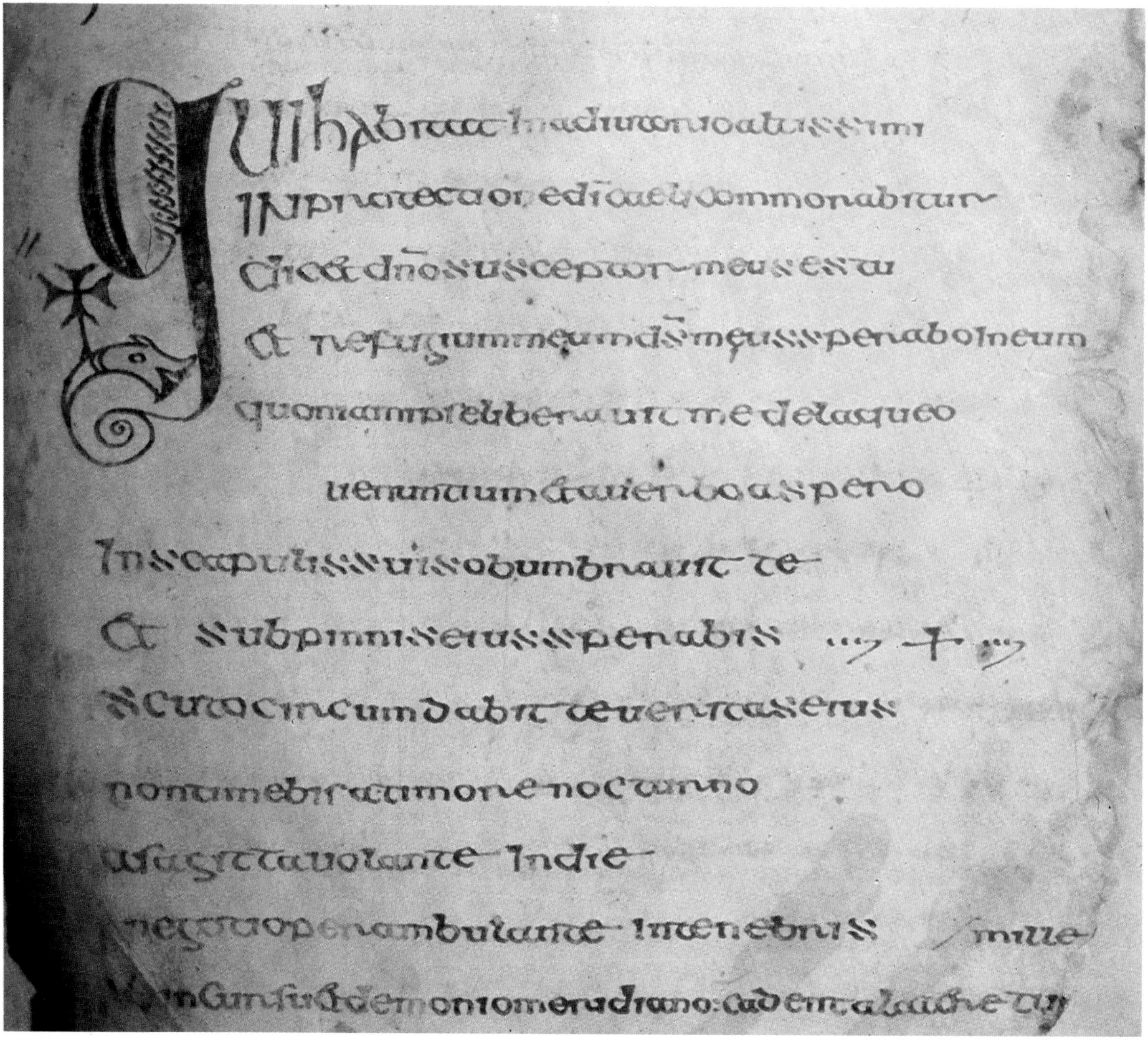

21. A page of a manuscript called the *Cathach,* which was written in Latin towards the end of the 6th century and is the earliest extant example of Irish manuscript writing.

22. Passage from the Book of Kells containing 'Patres nostri mannam manducaverunt . . .', the text used for a contrastive analysis of seventeenth-century Irish, Modern Irish, Scots Gaelic, and Manx at the end of Section II (page 53).

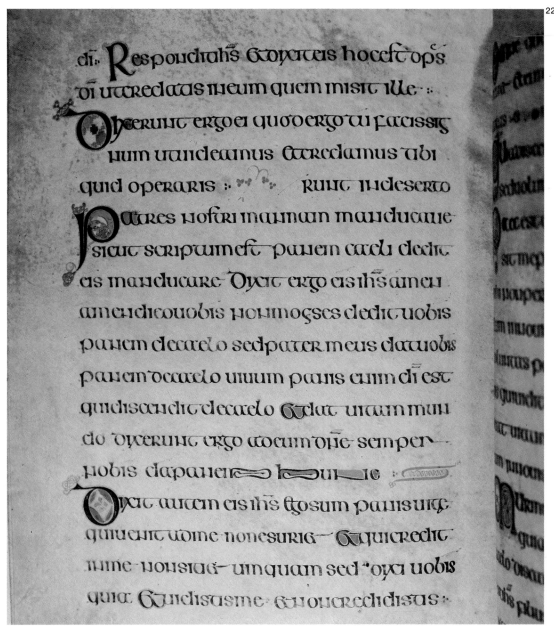

7. Emergence of an autonomous Manx

Prior to the 17th century, the Isle of Man would appear to have had a centre for native learning; Aodh Mac Aingil (1572-1626), briefly Roman Catholic Archbishop of Armagh, who wrote literary Irish with an easy elegance, received some of his education there. Yet, so abrupt was the change, when John Phillips arrived there as Anglican bishop in 1605 he encountered no trace of the native tradition of literacy and oversaw the production of a Manx translation of the Book of Common Prayer, completed around 1610, in an orthography based largely on English convention but with some Welsh influence. Needless to say, this new orthography is the medium for a distinctly local form of language and, to the extent that Manx has had a literary tradition since the 17th century, it has been quite autonomous of the other branches of the Gaelic tradition.

A brief illustration may be in order. John Cap. VI 31 appears in Manx as follows:

(i)
D'ee ny ayraghyn ain manna ayns yn aasagh; myr te scruit, Hug eh daue arran veih niau dy ee.
'Our fathers ate manna in the desert; as is written, He gave them manna from heaven to eat'.

In later editions of Uilliam Ó Domhnuill's *Tiomna Nuadh* (New Testament), this is:

(ii)
D'itheadar ar n-aithre-ne manna air an bhfásach; mar atá sgríobhtha, Thug sé arán ó neamh dhóibh ré na ithe.

D'itheadar is a 3rd person plural inflection to concord with the plural *aithre* 'fathers'; *aithre* is a conservative form, the Modern Irish *aithreacha* was also accepted in the Early Modern norm.

In Scots Gaelic the verse is as follows:

(iii)
Dh'ith ar n-aithrichean mana 's an fhàsach; a réir mar tha e sgrìobhtha, Thug a dhoibh aran o
nèamh r'a itheadh.

In *An Bíobla Naofa,* published under the auspices of the Irish Roman Catholic hierarchy in 1981, the contemporary Irish version is:

(iv)
D'ith ár n-aithreacha manna san fhásach faoi mar atá scríofa: 'Thug sé arán ó neamh dóibh le hithe'.

It can be observed at a glance that (i) belongs to a different convention from that of (ii), (iii) and (iv). Yet, the strange spelling in (i) conceals a form of language which is not all that divergent from the others (see Table 9). In particular, it must be noted that all modern versions use the non-personal form of the verb *d'ith* with a plural noun, instead of the more classical usage illustrated in (ii); this is an example of a grammatical change which, probably in the Early Modern period, occurred in the spoken tradition without divergence. In general, though, the language of Man was closer to Scottish varieties than to any variety in Ireland and this is seen in the form of the plural *ayraghyn/ aithrichean,* phonetically very similar in both, and in the form of the pronoun *eh/a* in contrast with the Irish *sé.* In the Manx version, possession is expressed by the construction *ny ayraghyn ain,* literally 'the fathers by us'; this construction, in Irish spelling *na haithreacha againn,* is found in all varieties but, again, is much more frequently used in Scotland than in Ireland as the ordinary expression of possession.

Since the 17th century Manx has suffered an even greater decline than Irish and Scots Gaelic and, although it is still learned as a second language, it had ceased to be a community language by the middle of the 20th century.

Table 9 A detailed comparison of the variants of *John* Cap. VI 31

1. 17th Century Irish	2. Modern Irish	3. Scots Gaelic	4. Manx	Commentary
d'itheadar	d'ith	dh'ith	d'ee	'ate'; 1. has a 3rd plural inflection in concord with the plural subject.
ar n-aithre-ne	ár n-aithreacha	ar n-aithrichean	ny ayraghyn ain	'our fathers'; 1. has emphatic suffix -ne meaning 'our fathers'; the other forms are non-emphatic.
air an bhfásach	san fhásach	's an fhàsach	ayns yn aasagh	'in the desert'; 1. means literally 'on the desert'; lenited f is silent and is not expressed in 4.
manna	manna	mana	manna	'manna';
mar atá	faoi mar atá	a réir mar tha	myr te	'as is'; 2. and 3. use longer expressions = 'according as'.
sgríobhtha	scríofa	sgrìobhtha	scruit	'written'; Mod. Irish is in the new simplified spelling; Manx has a reconstructed inflection of a kind also found in other regional varieties.
thug sé	thug sé	thug a	hug eh	'he gave'; th pronounced as h in all modern variants, is so written in 4.
arán ó neamh	arán ó neamh	aran o nèamh	arran veih niau	'bread from heaven'; Sc. Gaelic divergently has a long vowel in nèamh.
dhóibh	dóibh	dhoibh	daue	'to them'; the position of the word in the sentence varies, but without special significance.
ré na ithe	le hithe	r'a itheadh	dy ee	'to eat'; 1. and 3. mean literally 'for its eating'; 2. and 4. using different prepositions mean 'for eating'; Sc. Gaelic has regularised the verbal noun ending to -adh.

8. Summary

In summary, the complex pattern of chronological and regional variants of the Irish language may be portrayed diagrammatically as follows:

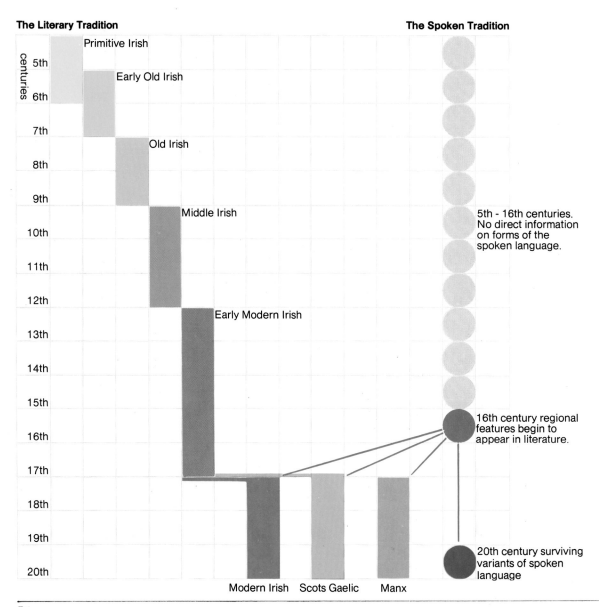

The Literary Tradition

The Spoken Tradition

centuries

5th — Primitive Irish
6th — Early Old Irish
7th
8th — Old Irish
9th
10th — Middle Irish
11th
12th
13th — Early Modern Irish
14th
15th
16th
17th
18th
19th
20th

Modern Irish   Scots Gaelic   Manx

5th - 16th centuries. No direct information on forms of the spoken language.

16th century regional features begin to appear in literature.

20th century surviving variants of spoken language

23. Though most famous for its large illuminations, the calligraphy throughout the Book of Kells is of outstanding quality as this passage from St Mark shows. The script is in the Irish majuscule style, which differs from the minuscule style which came to be associated exclusively with the writing of Irish.

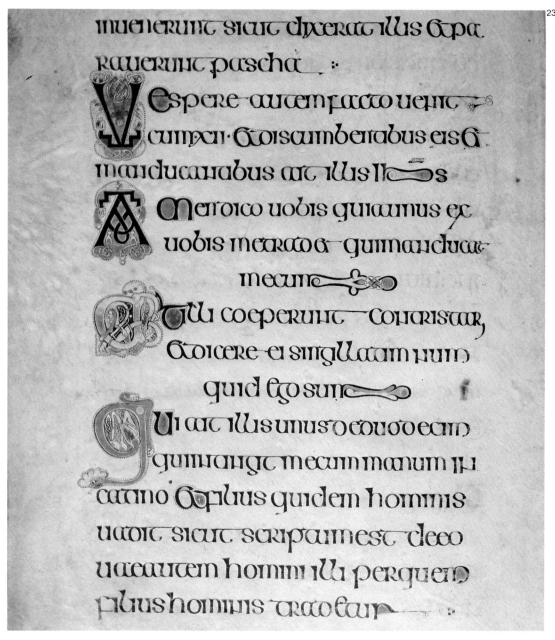

1. An Outline of Irish Grammar

I   Sentence Structure

1. The word order of the basic declarative sentence in Irish is Verb - Subject - Object, VSO for short. Corresponding to the English:

God (subject) *created* (verb) *heaven and earth* (object).
Irish has:
Chruthaigh (verb) *Dia* (subject) *neamh agus talamh* (object).

Irish shares this feature of word order with other modern Celtic languages, though there is evidence that the word order was different in earlier varieties of Celtic including Early Old Irish.

2. The verb need not be the absolutely first word of the declarative sentence; in addition to preverbal particles, it may be preceded by adverbials of time:
ansin chruthaigh Dia neamh agus talamh
i.e. 'then God created heaven and earth'.

II   The Verb Phrase

1. The verb may be preceded by various particles. For example, corresponding to the positive:
thóg fear airgead
took man money i.e. 'a man took money'

one may have:
níor thóg fear airgead
not + Past took man money i.e. 'a man did not take money'

ar thóg fear airgead
Interrogative + Past *took man money* i.e. 'did a man take money'

2. The verbal form is inflected for tense (time reference) and mood (attitudinal reference). For example, corresponding to the past tense positive:
thóg fear airgead
take + Past man money i.e. 'a man took money'

one may have:
thógadh fear airgead
take + Habitual Past man money i.e. 'a man used to take money'

tógann fear airgead
take + Present man money i.e. 'a man takes money'

tógfaidh fear airgead
take + Future man money i.e. 'a man will take money'

thógfadh fear airgead
take + Conditional man money i.e. 'a man would take money'

tógadh fear airgead
take + Imperative man money i.e. 'let a man take money'

3. Verbal forms may be inflected for person i.e. may express the actor by changes to their endings:

thógas airgead
take + Past + 1st person singular money i.e. 'I took money'

thógais airgead
take + Past + 2nd person singular money i.e. 'you (singular) took money'

thógadar airgead
take + Past + 3rd person plural money i.e. 'they took money'

4. In most instances, such inflected forms may be replaced by the non-personal form of the verb followed by an independent pronoun:

thóg mé airgead
take + Past + I money i.e. 'I took money'

thóg tú airgead
take + Past you (singular) *money* i.e. 'you took money'

thóg siad airgead
take + Past they money i.e. 'they took money'

This type of construction is predominant in the

modern language.

III   The noun phrase

1. The noun may be preceded by the definite article.
For example, corresponding to:

thóg fear airgead
take + Past *man money* i.e. 'a man took money'

one may have:
thóg an fear airgead
took the man money i.e. 'the man took money'

thóg an fear an t-airgead
took the man the money i.e. 'the man took the money'

thóg fear an t-airgead
took man the money i.e. 'a man took the money'

2. Adjectives normally follow the noun:

thóg fear mór an t-airgead
took man big the money i.e. 'a big man took the money'

thóg an fear mór láidir an t-airgead
took the man big strong the money i.e. 'the big strong man took the money'

3. Attributive nouns (in the genitive inflection) follow nouns which they qualify:

thóg an fear an t-airgead cíosa (:*cíos* 'rent')
took the man the money rent (attributive form) i.e. 'the man took the rent money'

4. If the attributive noun is defined by the article then the head noun cannot be so defined:

thóg an fear airgead na mná
took the man money the (genitive) *woman* (genitive) i.e. 'the man took the woman's money'

thóg fear an ghunna an t-airgead cíosa
took man the (genitive) *gun* (genitive) *the money*

rent (genitive) i.e. 'the gunman took the rent money'

5. A few adjectives are prefixed to the noun which they qualify e.g. *sean-* 'old':

thóg an seanfhear an t-airgead
took the old man the money i.e. 'the old man took the money'

6. Nouns are inflected for plural:

thóg fir an t-airgead
took man + plural *the money* i.e. 'men took the money'

7. The definite article and adjectives which qualify plural nouns are also marked for plural:

thóg na fir mhóra an t-airgead
took the (plural) *men big* (plural) *the money* i.e. 'the big men took the money'

IV   Prepositional phrases

1. The predicate of the sentence may be expanded by the addition of a prepositional phrase:

thóg an fear an t-airgead ó bhean
took the man the money from woman i.e. 'the man took the money from a woman'

thóg an fear an t-airgead ó na páistí beaga i.e. 'the man took the money from the little children'

2. If the prepositional phrase is represented by a preposition + pronoun, then a special form of the preposition inflected for person is used:

thóg an fear an t-airgead uaim
took the man the money from-me i.e. 'the man took the money from me'

thóg an fear an t-airgead uait
took the man the money from-you (singular) i.e. 'the man took the money from you'

V Copula and substantive verb

1. There is a grammatical distinction between statements of classification or identification using the copula *is* and expressions of state or condition using the substantive verb *tá*:

is bádóir an fear
is (copula) *boatman the man* i.e. 'the man is a boatman'

tá an fear i mbád
is (substantive) *the man in boat* i.e. 'the man is in a boat'

2. Classification can also be expressed by the following constructions:

bádóir is ea an fear
'boatman is (copula) it the man' i.e. 'the man is a boatman'

tá an fear ina bhádóir
is (substantive) *the man in his boatman* i.e. 'the man is a boatman'

The second of these constructions has some connotation of state or condition, suggesting what the subject has become or what his occupation is, but in some regions it is used, without this connotation, as the normal classificatory construction.

VI Special substantive verb constructions

1. The substantive verb *tá* is used in constructions with sets of nouns to express (a) conditions and (b) attitudes (which in English are more normally expressed by verbs):

(a) *tá áthas orm*
is joy on-me i.e. 'I am pleased'

tá dochma orm
is displeasure on-me i.e. 'I am displeased'

tá eagla orm
is fear on-me i.e. 'I am afraid'

tá ionadh orm
is wonder on-me i.e. 'I am surprised'

(b) *tá grá agam*
is love by-me i.e. 'I love'

tá gráin agam
is detestation by-me i.e. 'I detest'

tá fuath agam
is hatred by-me i.e. 'I hate'

tá meas agam
is respect by-me i.e. 'I respect'

tá trua agam
is pity by-me i.e. 'I pity'

Striking though these constructions may be for English speakers, they scarcely warrant the conclusion to which they sometimes give rise, that Irish is a noun-centred language.

VII Progressive constructions with the substantive verb

1. The various forms of the verb *tá* are used to express progressive aspects of the verb:

tá an fear ag tógáil airgid
is the man at taking money i.e. 'the man is taking money'

Since *tógáil* is grammatically a noun, its attributive noun *airgead* 'money' is in the genitive case, *airgid;* lit. 'at taking of money'.

2. The inflections of the verb *tá* provide a progressive aspect for all tenses and moods.
For example:

bhí an fear ag tógáil airgid
be + Past *the man at taking money* i.e. 'the man was taking money'

beidh an fear ag tógáil airgid
be + Future *the man at taking money* i.e. 'the man will be taking money'

Next page
24. Part of an Irish phrasebook compiled for the use of Queen Elizabeth I by Christopher Nugent, the 9th Baron of Delvin.

25. A page from Charlotte Brooke's *Reliques of Irish Poetry*, containing a section of the Ossianic poem *Laoi na Seilge* ('The Ballad of the Hunt').

3. Irish has an aspectual distinction between present *habitual* and present *punctual* in the substantive verb and this allows an equivalent distinction in the progressive which cannot readily be expressed in English.

tá an fear ag tógáil an airgid
is (punctual) *the man at taking the money* i.e. 'the man is (just now) taking the money'

bíonn an fear ag tógáil an airgid
is (habitual) *the man at taking the money* i.e. 'the man is (habitually) taking the money'

Not unnaturally this was felt by Irish-English bilinguals as a gap in the verbal system of English. The gap was filled by the construction *does be*, which has become a well-known feature of Irish English:

'the man does be taking money' i.e. the subject is engaged in the activity from time to time.

VIII   Inversions of the basic word order
1. The basic word order of sentences may, in constructions with the copula, be altered in various ways for contrastive emphasis.
For example, corresponding to the basic:

thóg fear an t-airgead ón bpáiste
took man the money from the child i.e. 'a man took the money from the child'

one may have:
is fear a thóg an t-airgead ón bpáiste
is (copula) *man that* (relative) *took the money from the child*

This is expressed in Irish English as:
''t is a man took the money from the child'

2. Any word in the sentence may similarly be brought forward:

is é an t-airgead a thóg an fear ón bpáiste
is it the money that took the man from the child i.e. ''t is the money the man took from the child'

is ón bpáiste a thóg an fear an t-airgead
is from the child that took the man the money i.e. ''t is from the child the man took the money'

is é an páiste ar thóg an fear an t-airgead uaidh
is he the child that + Past *took the man the money from-him* i.e. ''t is the child the man took the money from'

IX   Initial mutations
1. It will have been noticed that the beginnings of words change according to their grammatical meanings and environments:

tógann fear an t-airgead ó fhear eile (f ~ fh)
'a man takes the money from another man'

thóg fear an t-airgead: (thóg ~ tógann)
'a man took the money'

These are two examples of the initial mutation called *lenition*. Broadly speaking, lenition changes stop consonants to the corresponding fricatives, e.g. *p* changes to *f*, spelled in this context *ph; b* changes to *v*, spelled in the context *bh;* and so on.

2. The other important initial mutation is called eclipsis. Broadly speaking, it changes voiceless stop consonants *(p t c)* to the corresponding voiced consonants *(b d g* spelled *bp dt gc* in this context*)* and voiced stop consonants to the corresponding nasal consonants *(m n ng,* spelled *mb nd ng* in this context*)*; eclipsis changes *f* to *v*, spelled *bhf* in this context. For example:

thóg an fear an t-airgead ón bpáiste (:*páiste* 'child') 'the man took the money from the child'

thóg an fear an t-airgead ón bhfear eile (:*fear* 'man') 'the man took the money from the other man'

Iryſhe,	Latten,	Engliſhe,
Coneſ ta tu,	Quomodo habes,	How doe you.
Taim ʒo maih,	Bene ſum.	I am well,
ʒo ꝑo maih aʒaꝺ,	Habeo gratias,	I thancke you
In tolorꝺ ʒealaʒ ꝺo lauaiꝑꝺ,	Poſſis ne hibernice loqui,	Cann you speake Iryſh
A baiꞃ laꝺꝺen.	Dic latine.	Speake Latten
Dia leꝑiuean ꝑaxona	Deus adiuat Reginā Angliæ	God saue the Queene off Englande:

(283)

Aip bað an ojp do bj axolc
map peulc ajp apojż do bj
'xa paðpnjż da byajcxea aðpeað
do beapça do xeapc don mnaoj.
Dpproeaj fjonn aż jappajð xżèrl
ajp mnaoj xejmh na ccpáċ nòjp
Dxjaxpajż mo pjż don żnủjż nżil
an byacajð cr mo chojn xa cojp?
Ann do xejlż nj xbril mo xpejx.
Ij nj xhaca mé do ðá chojn
a Ržj na xejne żan cáp
Ij meaxa ljom xáċ mo żril
An è do čèjle do xuajp bàx
a jnżean clajè, no do mac
no cað è an xáċ xa byril do ċjój
ajnojp cójm Ij ájlne opeach
No cað ax abxril do bpón
a ajnnjp óż na mboj mjín
no an xèjojn cxuptacht (xj xjonn)
Ij ðubach ljom do bejċ map chjm
fájl ojp do bj xo mo żlajc
do pájð jnżean óż na byolc xejm
cxcjm dom lajm xan cxpeab
aż xjn maðbap da bejċ jbpèjn
Żeaxa map xbrlajnż laoch
cxrpjm do cjonn a Ržj na byhján
map ccużajp mchajmne cużam cajp ax
cxc pe beax na xpeab noján
Njop xhulajnż fjonn cup na nżeax
cpáċ cxrp ðe apajð xo na cnejj żlèjl
cuajð żo bpuað an loċa xnám
xj xhupajleam nina na mbaxx péjò.

O o 2   Do

2. A History of Irish Spelling

I Letters and their values

The letters of the Roman alphabet used in Irish spelling are:

a b c d e f g h i l m n o p r s t u v

Other letters such as *j k q x z* have some peripheral uses but are not essential to the convention.

The phonetic values of these letters are roughly as follows:

a e i o u represent short vowels somewhat similar, respectively, to the vowels in: *bat* (in Northern British accents), *bet, bit, homme* (French), *put; á é í ó ú* represent corresponding long vowels: the consonantal system is more complex than, for example, the consonantal system of any variety of English but it will not prejudice the present discussion to take the consonantal letters as having their English values, with the following qualifications:

c is in all environments pronounced as *k;*
ch ph th, for the earlier language, are as in *loch, pheasant, thin* but in the later period *th* is pronounced *h;*
bh dh gh represent the corresponding voiced sounds i.e. *bh* is pronounced as *v, dh* as *th* in *mother, gh* as *g* in Spanish *agua;* but in the later period *dh* came to be pronounced as *gh,* and many other phonetic changes affected the values which these digraphs now have;
fh is silent;
sh has the sound *h;*
mh represents the sound *v* but with the contiguous vowel being nasalized, as in French *vin.*

II The Orthography of Old Irish

The development of a writing system for Irish using the letters of the Roman alphabet must have been completed by the end of the 6th century AD though, as we have seen, the earliest extant contemporary records date from more than a century later. The more distinctive and, perhaps more bewildering, features of Irish orthography can be traced to the system then devised.

The phonetic value which the Roman letters were to have appears, at least in part, to have been determined by the correspondences which obtained between the spoken British Latin, with which the Irish were in contact, and traditional Latin orthography. Thus, for the British and Irish, in the spelling *scribo* b had the value of *v,* in *modus* d had the value of *th* in *mother,* in *lego* g had the value of *g* in Spanish *agua,* in *daemon* m had the value of *v* but with a nasalized vowel. Similarly, in *ecclesia* c(c) corresponds to a *g* sound, in *pater* t corresponded to a *d* sound, and in *operem* p corresponded to a *b* sound. On the other hand, when they occurred at the beginning of a word all of these letters had what, for simplicity, we might call their normal values. In *populus,* for example, the first *p* corresponded to a *p* sound but the internal *p* corresponded to a *b* sound. The early Irish monks transferred this rather complicated pattern of letter values into Old Irish spelling. The result was that Old Irish orthography does not unambiguously distinguish between *p - b, t - d* etc. sounds in the middle or end of words. For example, in *at* 'swelling' *t* represents a *t* sound, but in *gat* 'withe' *t* represents a *d* sound. Nor is the distinction betwen *b* and *v* etc. conveyed at the beginning of words. For example, *a bó* can represent a pronunciation in which *b* has a *v* sound and means 'his cow', or a pronunciation in which *b* has a *b* sound and means 'her cow'.

The phrase *a bó* involves the presence or absence of *lenition* and the inadequacies of the orthography, in effect, meant that it was not possible in all contexts to express this important initial mutation. The lenition of *c p t* was expressed by the use of the digraphs *ch ph th* available from Latin orthography e.g. *cat* 'cat': *mo chat* 'my cat'; *popul* 'people': *mo phopul* 'my people'; *tech* 'house': *mo thech* 'my house'. There was no corresponding mode of expressing the lenition of *b d g m* and consequently, as we have seen, *a bó* is ambiguous.

Lenition elides *f* and changes *s* to a *h* sound. These mutations were expressed by use of the *punctum delens,* a device used in Latin manuscripts to indicate that letters written in error should not be read: thus *fáilte* 'welcome', *ind fáilte* 'the welcome'; *sétig* 'wife', *a sétig* 'his wife'.

The other important initial mutation, *eclipsis,* was not adequately expressed either. The eclipsis of *b d g* was readily conveyed by writing *mb nd ng,* but the change of *c* to *g, p* to *b,* and *t* to *d* was not expressed at all. Thus *a gabur* 'her goat' is distinguished from *a ngabur* 'their goat', but the spelling *a cat* might stand for 'her cat' in which *c* represents a *k* sound, or 'their cat' in which *c* represents a *g* sound.

On the other hand, as we have seen in the case of *a bó, a gabur* might also represent a pronunciation in which *g* is a fricative, like *g* in Spanish *agua,* and mean 'his goat', while *a chat* 'his cat' is unequivocal. The following table provides a more schematic statement of these rather confusing facts:

c - initial	g - initial	mutation	
a cat	a gabur	no mutation	'her cat, goat'
a chat	a gabur	lenition	'his cat, goat'
a cat	a ngabur	eclipsis	'their cat, goat'

The most exotic feature of Old Irish pronunciation which the new orthography had to express was the contrast between slender consonants and broad consonants which by that period had developed in the middle and end of words. Slender consonants were distinguished from broad consonants by writing *i* after *u o a,* and sometimes after *e,* before the consonant letter. Thus *cat* 'cat' has broad *t, cait* 'cats' has slender *t;* the syllabic vowel *a* is the same in both cases. There is, however, a lacuna in the system: if the syllabic vowel is *i* (or *í*) no mode had been devised to express the contrast between broad and slender consonants and *min,* for example, could represent two pronunciations: with broad *n* meaning 'little', or with slender *n* meaning 'meal'.

III The Early Modern Orthography

Over the centuries the anomalies of the Old Irish spelling system were gradually rectified:

(i) *b d g m* acquired their normal values in the middle and end of words. This was made possible by using, on the pattern of *ch ph th,* the digraphs *bh dh gh mh* to represent the corresponding voiced consonants (*v* etc.).

(ii) Eclipsis of *c p t* was expressed by writing the initial consonant double or by prefixing the appropriate voiced consonant letter e.g. *a cat* 'their cat' was superseded by *a ccat* or *a gcat.* The table of mutations set out in Section 2 above would now have the following form:

c - initial	*g* - initial	mutation	
a cat	*a gabhar*	no mutation	'her cat, goat'
a chat	*a ghabhar*	lenition	'his cat, goat'
a gcat	*a ngabhar*	eclipsis	'their cat, goat'

(iii) The expression of the contrast between broad and slender consonants received further refinement. After *i* or *í* the letter *o* was written to express the broad quality in succeeding consonants e.g. *mion* 'little' with broad *n* in contrast to *min* 'meal' with slender *n*. Similarly, though with less necessity, *a* was written after *e, é* to mark the broad quality e.g. *fér* 'grass' was replaced by *féar.*

Although all features of the Early Modern orthography had made their appearance by the end of the 14th century, they were not consistently practised by the majority of scribes until they had been exemplified in the first printed books which, surprisingly in the circumstances, applied them with a high degree of regularity. Throughout most of the Early Modern period, the spelling of texts generally displayed considerable fluctuation between the Old Irish convention and the principles which had later developed. Yet a systematic appreciation of the new principles must have existed among the literary class. This is clear from the work of some scribes and scholars and, more especially, from the fact that they were so consistently applied in the first printed books by authors of differing backgrounds and working in different situations. The first book to be printed in the language was John Carswell's *Foirm na n-Urrnaidheadh* (1567), followed by Seán Ó Kearnaigh's *Aibidil Gaoidheilge & Caiticiosma* (1571), Uilliam Ó Domhnuill's *Tiomna Nuadh* (1603), and the various publications of the Franciscans in Louvain beginning with Giollabrighde Ó hEodhasa's *An Teagasg Criosdaidhe* (1611).

All of the books printed in Irish during this period were produced in response to the religious controversies of the time. For all that, they must have been widely studied as their normative

Table 10

A comparison between the Old Irish and Early Modern Irish spelling systems

Old Irish	Early Modern	
(i) the distinction of *p-b* etc.:		
popul	*pobal*	'people'
pater	*paidear*	'prayer'
cat	*cat*	'cat'
gat	*gad*	'withe'
eclais	*eaglais*	'church'
(ii) the distinction of *b-v* etc.:		
scrib	*sgríobh*	'write'
in bó	*an bhó*	'the cow'
mod	*modh*	'manner'
lég	*léagh*	'read'
demon	*deamhan*	'demon'
(iii) expression of consonant quality:		
min	*mion*	'little'
min	*min*	'meal'
síl	*síol*	'seed'
síl	*síl*	'seed' (genitive)
fér	*féar*	'grass'

influence on the subsequent writing of Irish was extensive; manuscripts of the 17th and 18th centuries follow much more consistently the principles of the Early Modern orthography. Consequently, this inevitably became the orthography to be adopted when secular literature in Irish first began to appear in print towards the end of the 18th century. The first publication was Charlotte Brooke's *Reliques of Irish Poetry* (1789); thereafter publications grew in volume as the 19th century progressed, until the Irish revival activity of the late 19th and early 20th centuries produced a further rapid increase. Influential figures in the revival favoured the Early Modern norm and its conventions were codified and powerfully promoted by Patrick Dinneen's chaotic but immensely influential dictionary, first published in 1904 and again, in revised and enlarged form, in 1927.

IV The decline of the Early Modern Spelling Norm

Yet the first decades of the 20th century saw a decline in the stability of Irish orthography. This arose because, following the success of Peadar Ó Laoghaire's campaign to promote the 'speech of the people', there was an increased concern with the forms of the spoken language and a growing acceptance that the writer should 'give us the language exactly as he speaks it himself, and as he hears it from the best native speakers'. In this situation writers, who felt that a faithful adherence to the forms of the spoken language ought to be reflected in spelling as well as in grammar and vocabulary, began variously to modify the received spelling which, in relation to pronunciation, was by now extremely cumbersome. The resultant uncoordinated and unsystematic attempts at modifying the spelling norm inevitably gave rise to a great deal of unnecessary variation, not only between texts but also within individual texts.

One of the more extreme developments during this period was the *Letiriú Shímplí* ('Simple Spelling'), a system of spelling put forward in 1910 by Osborn Bergin and Shán Ó Cuív with assistance from Richard O'Daly. This spelling was devised, in the first instance, with reference to the pronunciation of Irish in West Cork and at least some of its principles derive from English spelling. The following tables gives some indication of its character:

Letiriú Shímplí	Early Modern	Old Irish	
(i)			
by	buidhe	buide	'yellow'
cry	croidhe	cride	'heart'
dy	duibhe	duibe	'blackness'
ly	laighe	lige	'lying'
(ii)			
lí	lí	lí	'complexion'
shí	sídhe	síde	'fairy'
trí	trí	trí	'three'
(iii)			
sí	suidhe	suide	'sitting'

All of the words in these tables have the same vowel in the variety of Irish being represented here by the *Letiriú Shímplí*. In the first set the initial consonants are broad; in the second set the initial consonants are slender. The contrast is expressed by using *y* in the first set to represent the vowel and *i* to represent the same vowel in the second set. This scheme is not without a certain elegance. However, in the third set *sí*, the initial *s* is broad but the vowel is nevertheless spelled *i*, and this must be because the contrast in consonant quality can in this case be expressed by recourse to the English digraph *sh* for slender *s*. Thus we have *ly* - *lí* but *sí* - *shí*. This rather spoils the symmetry and demonstrates that the *Letiriú Shímplí* was in some ways an awkward system and scarcely simple in any objective sense. It was, in any case, too extreme a departure from the traditional orthography, as well as being too closely associated with one specific variety of the language, to have been widely adopted. Because of the prestige of those who promoted it, however, it must have helped to increase the instability of the Early Modern norm.

26. Two versions of the beginning of a text from Peadar Ó Laoghaire's collection of fables *Aesop a tháinig go hÉirinn* ('An Aesop who came to Ireland'). The first is from the edition of 1904 in Irish script and a rather personal variant of Early Modern spelling; the second is from Osborn Bergin's 1911 edition in the *Letiriú Shímpli*. The syntax of the title has been changed in the later edition.

8.—NA FROGANA A' LORG RÍGH.

Bhí loch breágh mór fairsing i lár machaire, agus é lán ó thaobh thaobh d'fhroganaibh. Frogana breághtha sleamhne beathuighthe b'eadh iad. Bhí cuid acu mór agus cuid acu beag, cuid acu óg agus cuid acu críona, cuid acu buidhe agus cuid acu crón. Acht beag agus mór dóibh, buidhe agus crón dóibh, óg agus críona dóibh, ní raibh oiread agus aon fhrog amháin acu go raibh buairt ná brón ná earba sláinte air. Ní raibh de ghnó ná d'obair ná de chúram orrtha, ó mhaidin go h-oidhche acht beith ag snámh anonn 's anall tríd an uisge, nó ag caitheamh trí léim táiliúra de dhruim achéile, nó 'gá n-iomlorg féin fá ghlótaig. Dar leó níor deineadh ceól ríghe riamh ba bhreághtha 'ná an ceól a bhíodh acu agus iad ag crónán agus ag cnádán agus ag cneadaig, mór tímpal an loca. Do cluintí an dórd reacht n-acra ó'n loch, i dtreó, nuair bíodh an mada ruadh nó an giorrfiadh ag teacht abaile ó'n bhfiadhach go ratadaidhir tamal ag éirteacht leir an bhfogar mbreágh.

8.—NA FROGANA ER LORAG RY.

Ví loch breá muar fairshing a lár machuiri, agus é lán ó häv täv do roganuiv. Frogana breáha shleâuini beahihi b'ea iad. Ví cuid acù muar agus cuid acù beog, cuid acù óg agus cuid acù críona, cuid acù by

5 agus cuid acù crón. Ach beog agus muar dóiv, by agus crón dóiv, óg agus críona ghóiv, ní roiv iread agus än rog aváin acù go roiv buert ná brón ná easba sláinti er. Ní roiv do ghnó ná d'obuir ná do chúram orha, ó vaidin go híhi, ach veh a snâv anún 's anaul

10 tríd an uishgi, nú a cahav trí lém táiliúra do ghruím a chéli, nú á n-umalosc fén sa ghlóhig. Dar leó níor dineag ceol shí ryav ba vreáha ná an ceol a víoch acù, agus iad a crónán agus a cnádán agus a cneaduig, mór hímpal a locha. Do cluintí an dórd shacht

15 n-acara ó'n loch, a dreo, nuer a víoch a mada rua nú an giorä a teacht aváili ó'n viach, go sdaduidísh tamal ag éshdeacht lesh a vour mreá.

At the other extreme there were the conservatives who held that, faced with the diversity of the spoken language, the received spelling was the best solution to the problem of maintaining a standardised orthography. This was the position of Dinneen: 'It is believed that the interests of simplicity as well as uniformity, a uniformity that affords a working basis even for dialectic variations, are best served by retaining the traditional orthography'. It was also the position maintained by L. Mac Cionnaith who edited the State-sponsored English-Irish dictionary which was published in 1935.

Middle ground was held by those who argued that the more redundant features of the Early Modern norm could be excised without abandoning its basic principles. This, for example, was the position of T. F. O'Rahilly, a leading Irish scholar in his day: 'Such cumbrous spellings as *beirbhiughadh* (for *beiriú*), *imthighthe* (for *imithe*), *faghbháil* (for *fáil*), *urradhas* (for *urrús*), and *filidheacht* (for *filíocht*) would be a severe handicap on any language, and are simply impossible in the case of Irish if we really mean to give it a fair chance of life'.

Diversity and instability were no more than a mild inconvenience while the cultivation of Irish was confined to the voluntary and zealous members of the revival movement. Such people were well equipped and highly motivated to cope with the complexities of an unstable orthography and to acquiesce in the belief that 'the exact representation of the words as they are uttered . . . will neither increase nor lessen the dialectal varieties existing, it will merely enable the reader to pronounce with certainty where he may now be in doubt, while sparing the writer a considerable amount of worse than useless labour'. This kind of *carte blanche* to writers became quite impractical after 1922 when the Irish State was attempting to promote the language in the public service and education. The need for a new and, if possible, simplified standard was fairly quickly recognised. Work on devising one had been officially begun by 1929 but, following a change of government in

1932, the effort faltered. The new administration initially found the conservative stance on spelling reform more compatible with its ideological position generally. The practical realities continued to make themselves felt, however, and reform got under way again around 1938 and was then pursued with vigour. Many scholars were consulted and a committee was established under the chairmanship of T. F. O'Rahilly, whose brief was to devise rules 'for abbreviating the spelling of Irish'. Unfortunately the membership of the committee was constituted to include a range of opinion and progress was frustrated by members who not only resolutely opposed reform but would, in O'Rahilly's judgement, have preferred to make Irish spelling more complicated if they could. The committee disbanded without agreeing recommendations but O'Rahilly set out his own guidelines and these formed the basis for further work which was undertaken by members of the translation section of the *Oireachtas* (Legislature) staff headed by Liam Ó Rinn and Tomás Page. Their recommendations were published in *Litriú na Gaeilge* in 1945 and again with revisions in 1947. Since 1958 the official spelling and grammatical norms have been published together in a single book.

V The New Spelling

The reforms proposed in *Litriú na Gaeilge* were essentially conservative; they represent a modification of the Early Modern norm rather than the establishment of a new one. Letters retained their previous values and the typical features of traditional Irish orthography were preserved. The reforms were of two kinds:

(i) In cases where usage had never been stabilised one particular variant was recommended e.g. that *a* rather than *o* or *u* be written in weakly stressed syllables, thus *easpag* 'bishop' rather than *easbog*, *solas* 'light' rather than *solus;* or that *c p t* rather than *b d g* be written after *s,* thus *easpag* 'bishop' rather than *easbog, scéal* 'story' rather than *sgéal* etc.

(ii) With respect to the Early Modern convention it

27 Entries in *Gearrfhoclóir Gaeilge-Bearla*, a shortened version of Niall O Dónaill's dictionary *Foclóir Gaeilge-Bearla*.

proposed that the spelling should be shortened in the case of words which had fewer syllables in the spoken language, or in the case of words which had more simple consonantal structures in the spoken language (see Table 11).

Table 11

A comparison of the Early Modern and later simplified spelling systems

Early Modern spelling	New spelling	
(i) representation of new monosyllables		
cuibhdhe	cuí	'(more) appropriate'
suidhe	suí	'sitting'
buidhean	buíon	'troop'
fighe	fí	'weaving'
feadha	feá	'wood'
(ii) reduction in number of unstressed syllables		
duilleabhar	duilliúr	'foliage'
bunadhas	bunús	'basis'
ardughadh	ardú	'raising'
ceanamhail	ceanúil	'affectionate'
sgéalaighe	scéalaí	'storyteller'
filidheacht	filíocht	'poetry'
(iii) simplification of consonantal structure		
adhbhar	ábhar	'matter'
foghnamh	fónamh	'functioning'
inghean	iníon	'daughter'
bradghail	bradail	'thieving'

The new spelling has remained largely unchanged since 1947. Its use spread rapidly. It was adopted immediately for official publications, then for school texts. It was confirmed by Tomás de Bhaldraithe's authoritative English-Irish dictionary published in 1959 and is now definitively codified in Niall Ó Dónaill's Irish-English dictionary published in 1978. There has, of course, been opposition to the new spelling, both from conservatives and more radical reformers, but it has been accepted by the majority as the most acceptable compromise between the various possible approaches to the reform of Modern Irish orthography.

Gaeilgeoireacht, *f.* (*gs.* ~a). (Act of) speaking Irish.

Gael, *m.* (*gs. & npl.* -eil, *gpl.* ~). **1.** Irishman, Irishwoman. **2.** (Scottish) highlander.

Gaelach, *a1.* **1.** Irish. **2.** Attached to Irish, to Irish culture. **3.** (*Usually with lower-case initial*) (*a*) Native to Ireland. (*b*) Homely, pleasant. (*c*) Common, ordinary.

Gaelachas, *m.* (*gs.* -ais). **1.** Irish characteristic(s). **2.** Attachment to Irish culture.

Gaelaigh, *v.t.* Gaelicize.

Gaeltacht, *f.* (*gs.* ~a, *pl.* ~aí). **1.** *Lit:* Irishry; Irish(-speaking) people. **2.** Irish-speaking area. **3.** Gaelic-speaking area of Scotland.

Gaelú, *m.* (*gs.* -laithe). Gaelicization.

gafa, *a3.* **1.** *pp.* of GABH. **2.** (*a*) Taken, caught, held. **Bheith** ~ **i ngreim** (**ag rud**), to be held in a grip (by sth.). ~ **i bpríosún**, held in prison. ~ **sa dris,** caught in the briar. (*b*) Gripped by infection. ~ **ag slaghdán,** in the grip of a cold. ~ **san ucht,** caught in the chest. (*c*) Occupied, absorbed, wholly engaged. **Bheith** ~ **in obair,** to be caught up, engrossed, in work. **Tá siad** ~ **ina chéile,** they are wrapped up in each other. **Ní bheinn** ~ **leis,** I wouldn't be bothered with it. (*d*) Engaged. **Tá an suíochán** ~, the seat is engaged. (*e*) *Mth:* Contained. **Tá B** ~ **in A,** A contains B. **3.** Fitted, harnessed; dressed, arrayed. ~ **gléasta,** (*of implement*) fitted and ready; (*of horse*) yoked and harnessed; (*of person*) all dressed up.

gafann, *f.* (*gs.* -ainne). Henbane.

gág[1], *f.* (*gs.* **gáige,** *npl.* ~a, *gpl.* ~). **1.** Crack, chink, crevice. **2.** Crack in skin, chap. **3.** Narrow creek. **4.** Thin leg.

gág[2], *v.t. & i.* (*vn.* ~adh *m, gs. & pp.* ~tha). Crack, chap.

gágach, *a1.* **1.** Cracked, fissured; chapped. *S.a.* MÁIRTÍN. **2.** Thin, measly, miserable.

gágaí, *f.* (*gs.* ~). Cracked, chapped, condition.

gágaire, *m.* (*gs.* ~, *pl.* -rí). Thin-legged person or animal.

28

28. A page containing part of chapter 20 of the Gospel according to St Matthew, from Uilliam Ó Domhnuill's *Tiomna Nuadh* (New Testament) published in Dublin in 1603.

CAP. 20.   17

an láoi do chup lochda oibpe ap pop-
máil an a fineamuin.

2 Agus tap éip péjoigte pip an lucho
oibpe ap ffingin pa ló, do chuip pé
an a fineamain jad.

3 Agus ap noul a mach dó tjmcheall
an tpeap uaip, do cofujc pé dpong
ejle ojmáojneach jona pearam ap an
mapgad.

4 Agus a dubaipt pé piu, imoigig lejp
don fineamain, agus giod bé nj búp
ceaph do bépa mé ojb [é.]

5 Agus do imoigeadappan. A píp ap
njmteacho a mach dó, tjmcheall an
pejpead agus an náomad húaip, do
pjpe pé map an gcéona.

6 Agus ap noul a mach dó a dtjmcheall
an áonmad húaip dég, puaip pé dpem
ejle jona pearam ojmáojneach, agus
a deip pé piu, cpéo joma bfujltjpj
jon bap pearam ap po pead an láoi
ojmáojneach?

7 A deipjo piadpan pip, ap pon nap
chongaim dujne ap bjod ap túapap-
dal pn. A deip pejpean piu, imoigigig
map an gcéona don fineamain, agus
giod bé nj búp cojp do gheubtháoj
[é.]

8 Agus ap dteacho don tpáth nóna a
deip tigheapna na fineamhna pé na
pojobapjo, goip an lucho oibpé, agus
tabaip dójb a dtúapapdal, ag topu-
gad ón lucho tájnjc pá dejpead, gu
pojte na céodáojne.

12 Agá pádá, an dpeampo tájnjc pa dejpead, nj deapnadap [obaip] acd áon-
úaip a mháin, ⁊ do chuippij a gcojm-
meap pijne, do jomchuip muipjojn a-
gus teaptach an láoj, jad.

13 Agus ap bfpeagpa dópan a dubaipt
pé pé peap djob, a chompánujg, nj
fujljm ag dénam égcópa opt : a né
nach ap péjoig tú pjom ap ffingin?

14 Tógajb leat do chujo péjn, agus
imoig, a pj mo tojlj a tabaipt don
téig tájnjc pá dejpead map [tug mé]
dujtjj.

15 A né nach ceadujgteach damja an nj
jp tojl leam péjn do dénam pém cyo
féjn? an bfujl do fujljj gu holc ap pó
gu bfujljmj majt?

16 Jp map pin bejo na [dáojne] thjg pa
dejpead a dtopach : agus na [dáoj-
ne] a tá a dtopac pa dejpead. Ojp jp
mór a tá ap na ngajpm, agus jp bég
a tá ap na dtoga.

17 Agus ag dul púap Dhjópa gu Hjá-
pupaléjm, pug pé an dá ojpgjobal
dég lejp pa leit ap pa tpljgjd, agus a
dubaipt pé piu,

18 Fécha támáojo ag dul púap gu Hjá-
pupaléjm, agus do béptbap mac an
dujne dúachdapánajb na pagapt ⁊
do doctúpajb an oljójd, agus béppo
pjad bpeat bájp ap:

19 ⁊ do béppujo pjad do na cjneadachujb
é do chum gu noéndáojp ponámad

3. A History of the Irish Script

1. In the earliest extant manuscripts Irish is written in letters, or characters, which were similar to those used in contemporary Latin writing. The style was, however, already distinctively Irish and, as the centuries passed, it grew increasingly divergent from the scripts which were evolving in Europe. Indeed, there would appear to have been a resistance to later European styles. Anglo-Norman influences, for example, appeared in the *Annals of Inisfallen* in the entry for the year 1197, less than thirty years after the Norman invasion, in the form of gothic characters for *f* and *s*. In some later periods in the same Annals (e.g. 1253-1273) entries are entirely in gothic script. Entries then reverted to exclusive use of the Irish style of writing, but the conflict had effected a fundamental change: the Irish style seems thereafter to have been perceived as a distinct alphabetic form associated excusively with writing the Irish language. Thus, in sections of the *Annals of Inisfallen* written in the 15th century, the convention of using the Irish style for the Irish language and the gothic style for Latin had been established. This contrasts with earlier parts of the *Annals* in which the Irish style is used both for Latin and Irish. In later manuscripts the norm was to use the Irish script for Irish and the contemporary roman script for quotations and names in Latin, English, and other languages.

2. John Carswell's translation of the Liturgy of John Knox was the first appearance of the language in print. It was printed in Edinburgh in 1567 and used the normal contemporary roman type. The first book in Irish to be published in Ireland was Seán Ó Kearnaigh's *Aibidil Gaoidheilge & Caiticiosma*. It was printed in Dublin in 1571 from a fount specially cut in London by order of Elizabeth I. For this fount, letters resembling those of Irish manuscript style were cut for *d e f g i p r s t* which, apart from *p,* were the most distinctive in the Irish script. For the rest, a mixture of italic and roman characters was used, but the overall visual effect is of Irish manuscript writing and so the concept of a distinctive Irish script was carried into print. Uilliam Ó Domhnuill's

Tiomna Nuadh (1603) was also printed from this fount. Why it was felt desirable by Elizabeth I and her officials to reproduce the Irish characters in print is not entirely clear. It may have been because it was distinctive enough to have been regarded as an essential part of the language, as many in the 19th and 20th centuries certainly felt it to be. Either the authorities were not aware of the Carswell precedent or believed it was not relevant to the situation in Ireland.

After the type made for Elizabeth I, the next Irish fount was cut by the Franciscans in Louvain for printing counter-reformational material. Their first publication was Giollabrighde Ó hEodhasa's *An Teagasg Criosdaidhe* which appeared in 1611. The Franciscans' type was an even more exact replication of Irish manuscript writing than that of Elizabeth I and must have helped to reinforce the concept of a distinctive Irish type. At any rate, the Franciscans' example was closely followed in the few new founts which were made for Irish between 1611 and the end of the 18th century, when a new fount of Irish characters was made for Charlotte Brooke's *Reliques of Irish Poetry.* In the 19th century further new Irish types were produced and one or two of them were especially attractive; for example, one made by Petrie in 1841 and one made by Thom in 1862. In the present century another attractive Irish type was designed by Colm Ó Lochlainn.

3. The *punctum,* which initially in Irish orthography was used to express the lenition of *f* and *s* and later was used in free variation with *h* in various digraphs, began increasingly in the printed texts of the 19th century to replace *h* altogether. By the end of the century, when the Irish revival was giving rise to a good deal of publishing in Irish, the *punctum* had completely ousted *h* and had come to be regarded as an integral feature of the Irish script. The use of *h,* on the other hand, was regarded as the appropriate substitute for the *punctum* when roman type was being used. This was perhaps an unfortunate development for the Irish script because, in printing, it required it to have nine additional typefaces to express the nine

abcdefgh
ilmnoprs
tu

abcoefghij
klmnopqrs
tuvwxyz

consonant letters which might combine with the *punctum,* thus making it considerably less economical and less practical.

At the beginning of the revival period, the Irish script had great symbolic force. E. W. Lynam, an eminent authority on its history in print, expressed the opinion of many when he wrote: 'Anyone who is familiar with Irish in the Irish character will find not only difficulty but annoyance in reading it in Roman type. The language loses much of its individuality, just as Greek does in Roman type'. Despite such attachment to the Irish type, there was an inevitable pressure to abandon it for the roman. Roman type was universally available, a fact which was increasingly important as routine printing in the language grew. Then, after the foundation of the State, roman type greatly facilitated the printing of bilingual forms and documents and, at the most utilitarian level, meant that State departments did not have to bear the cost of two sets of typewriters.

4. Roman type began, therefore, to be used extensively in the Irish publications of the new State. It was, of course, the subject of much debate and much vacillation. When, for example, L. Mac Cionnaith was preparing his English-Irish dictionary, his first instructions were that it be produced in roman type, but these were subsequently reversed and, in the event, Irish type was used for Irish in it. MacCionnaith's description of developments is interesting: 'In the earlier stages of our work we used roman letters, being instructed so to do. In order to avoid the unsightliness of multidudinous "h's" and also in order to conform to much weighty and authoritative advice, we drew up a fairly extensive system of simplified spelling. The progress of our work, however, entailing as it did constant comparisons of the various dialects, brought home to us very forcibly the difficulties involved in any system of simplified spelling which would do equal justice to all the dialects. Little by little our projected simplifications had to be discarded. When, subsequently, we had received instructions to adopt the Irish letters, the reasons for any

SELF-INSTRUCTION IN IRISH.

THE ALPHABET.

The Alphabet of the Irish Language has but seventeen letters, which are called 𝔄ıbᵹıꞇın na Ᵹaoıðeılᵹe (i.e. the Alphabet of the Irish Language), and are expressed in the following Table :—

CAPITALS. Eng.	CAPITALS. Irish	SMALL LETTERS. Eng.	SMALL LETTERS. Irish	IRISH NAMES.	DERIVATION.
A	𝔄	a	a	𝔄ılım	Palm
B	B	b	b	Beıꞇ	Birch
C	C	c	c	Coll	Hazel
D	Ꝺ	d	ꝺ	Ꝺuın	Oak
E	E	e	e	Eaða	Aspen
F	F	f	f	Feaꞃan	Alder
G	Ᵹ	g	ᵹ	Ᵹoꞃꞇ	Ivy
I	J	i	ı	Joða	Yew
L	L	l	l	Luıꞃ	Quicken
M	𝔐	m	m	𝔐uın	Vine
N	N	n	n	Nuın	Ash
O	O	o	o	Oıꞃ	Broom
P	P	p	p	Peıꞇ	Dwarf-elder
R	R	r	ꞃ	Ruıꞃ	Elder
S	S	s	ꞅ	Suıl	Willow
T	Ꞇ	t	ꞇ	Ꞇeıne	Furze
U	U	u	u or v	Uꞃ	Heath

simplified system of spelling seemed less urgent, and finally we reverted almost completely to the literary or Dinneen spelling'. There can be little doubt about where Mac Cionnaith's heart lay and we see clearly in his statement how the essentially unrelated questions of spelling reform and of type had become interdependent. Early Modern spelling and the Irish script would stand or fall together.

The change of instructions to Mac Cionnaith occurred after there had been a change of government in 1932. The new government favoured the Irish script, as it favoured the traditional spelling, but when it came to appreciate the practicalities it abandoned both. The new spelling handbook, published in 1945 and 1947, was in roman type and, thereafter, official use of Irish type lapsed, except in the sphere of education. There was some hesitation about promoting the roman type in schools but, eventually, the inevitable decision was taken and roman type had been introduced to all classes in primary schools by 1964 and to all classes in secondary schools by 1970. Use of the Irish script is now rare.

Select Bibliography

1. Grammar, Linguistics, and Writing
H. d'Arbois de Jubainville, *Eléments de la Grammaire Celtique.*
G. Dottin, *Manuel D'Irlandais Moyen.*
E. W. Lynam, *The Irish Character in Print* 1571-1923.
R. Thurneysen, *A Grammar of Old Irish.*
H. Wagner, *Linguistic Atlas and Survey of Irish Dialects.*

2. Social and Political History
M. Dillon and N. Chadwick, *The Celtic Realms.*
G. FitzGerald, *Estimates for Baronies of Minimum Level of Irish-speaking amongst Successive Decennial Cohorts: 1771-1781 to 1861-1871*
K. H. Jackson, *Language and History in Early Britain.*
B. Ó Cuív (ed.), *A View of the Irish Language.*
B. Ó Cuív, *Irish Dialects and Irish-speaking Districts*
G. Price, *The Languages of Britain.*
F. T. Wainwright (ed.), *The Problem of the Picts.*
W. J. Watson, *Celtic Placenames of Scotland.*
Ch. W. J. Withers, *Gaelic in Scotland* 1698-1981.

3. Instructional
  a. D. Ó Donnchadha, *Cúrsa Gaeilge,* Linguaphone/Gael-Linn.
  M. Dillon and D. Ó Cróinín, *Teach Yourself Irish,* English Universities Press.
  M. Ó Siadhail, *Learning Irish,* Dublin Institute for Advanced Studies.

  (Of these D. Ó Donnchadha is probably the most suitable for learners who have had no previous contact with Irish and do not have a teacher to guide them).

  b. T. de Bhaldraithe, *English-Irish Dictionary,* Stationery Office Dublin.
  N. Ó Dónaill, *Foclóir Gaeilge-Béarla* ('Irish-English Dictionary'), Stationery Office Dublin.

  c. Up to date information on learning materials may be obtained from:

The Librarian,
Institiúid Teangeolaíochta Éireann,
(Linguistics Institute of Ireland),
31 Fitzwilliam Place,
Dublin 2

or:
The Director,
Centre for Language and Communication Studies,
Trinity College,
Dublin 2.